A QUIET WORD

You hold in your hands a dangerous weapon, dear reader. One could bludgeon a man to death with a book.

This is true of the hardback, at least. The paperback is likely to cause little more than a sting to the man, and embarrassment to the bludgeoner.

However, when pulped and mixed with a man's porridge, the print held within may be enough to poison a man to death.

Before you enter this course of action, you may want to arm yourself with these thoughts:

The above actions are still frowned upon in some countries of the world.

and

You may wish to run these by a local law enforcement officer before proceeding.

WOMEN ON TOP 2

Women on Top 2
The Testicles

Daniel Silman & Sean Freeman

With an introduction by

Professor GC Cleftbottom

PRAISE FOR WOMEN ON TOP: A DUD'S TALE

"Dud Wimpole's words have a profoundly honest ring, for they rest on experiences too deep for deception... A gem of a dramatic narrative focused on the deepest of human problems."

Professor Gordon W. Allport

"*Women on Top: A Dud's Tale* might well be prescribed for everyone who would understand our time."

Journal of Individual Psychology

"An inspiring document of an amazing man who was able to garner some good from an experience so abysmally bad... Highly recommended."

Library Journal

"Studded with sharp assessments."

Washington Post

"As a healthy, middle aged woman, I like to indulge my natural rape fantasies by reading literature. This book was sorely lacking in regards to that end, and I do use "sorley" as a double entendre. *Women on Top: A Dud's Tale* contains very little in the way of graphic depictions of brutal love-play and next to nothing in terms of revelries in blood loss, nor creative ideas for the use of kitchen implements in the bedroom. As for Dud Wimpole, I doubt he could turn on a light switch!"

Grenada Smith

"Beautifully observed."

Slate

"I wet myself laughing. I cried with laughter. Then I wet myself crying."

Tamara Jackson

"A goldmine of surprising insights; makes you smarter with every page."

James Clear

"I bought this book for my wife, hoping it would expand her interests, and get her off the reality TV for a few minutes. From the pre order listing, I thought it was going to be about female empowerment. I figured there would be stuff to inspire a woman to take action.

Instead, it turned out to be about this Dud Wimpole character, an utterly useless nerd who couldn't do anything, and who seems to have this innate ability to annoy women. My wife read the first chapter and then she asked me to get out of the house.

What's more, while I was gone, she sold all my He-Man figures! How could this happen? - I can hear you ask. Well, leaving in a hurry as I did, I didn't have time to go into the garage and get the figures from the box in which I keep them. I had other things to worry about, like where was I going to sleep that night! (My brother let me sleep on his couch).

I'd assumed I'd only be out until the lady cooled off, anyway. She turned out to be so insulted by this book, and this Dud Wimpole character, that she NEVER cooled off. Instead, she texted me a week later saying that we were getting a divorce, and that I should collect my stuff.

I would have loved to collect my stuff - if she hadn't sold my entire collection of He-Man figures!!! The whole lot was gone! I had a near complete collection - except from Rotar and Twistoid - but I could have got them from somewhere, anyway.

I had three original He-Men, two in near mint collection, complete with weapons. There was a load of other weapons in there, too. Most of the figures were complete. In a separate box, there were some vehicles and a complete Castle Grayskull, too.

Let me be clear here. I'm not talking about the new Origins line or any of the other reboots. Not even Classics. I'm talking about the original, 1980s line that I'd had since childhood. You know, the one with sentimental value? Irreplaceable.

She went into the garage and sold it in the yard - and the neighbour says she was looking for $500 for it, even though a complete collection is going for ten times that much on ebay.

Each one of those figures had sentimental value. Some were impromptu gifts from school friends. Others were Christmas presents I'd waited all year for… Only good news - I'd got a commemorative Battle Armor He-Man and Skeletor set for my nephew, and those are at my brother's house, so those are safe.

But it's not the same.

Nothing is the same.

Not now.

Not ever again..."

Slim Neilhart

Available at Barnes and Noble:

https://www.barnesandnoble.com

For Dud

CONTENTS

WOMEN ON TOP 2: THE TESTICLES

Introduction   3

PART ONE: PEARLS   7

Chapter One: Someone With Nothing   9

Chapter Two: Enough About Me   17

Chapter Three: What Makes a Dud?   23

Chapter Four: The Beyonce Islands   27

Chapter Five: Dileag   35

Chapter Six: Appendix to Part One   41

PART TWO: WALNUTS   45

Chapter Seven: I Am Always Ready   47

Chapter Eight: I Know How to Control a Man   51

Chapter Nine: I Have Many Charming Quirks   57

Chapter Ten: I'm Fifty Shades of Hot   63

Chapter Eleven: I Deserve More   69

Chapter Twelve: I'm a Strong and Capable Woman   77

Chapter Thirteen: I Am Perfectly Stable   83

Chapter Fourteen: I Am on the Cusp of Greatness   89

Chapter Fifteen: I Am a Star   95

Chapter Sixteen: I Am a Woman on Top   101

PART THREE: GRENADES 107

Chapter Seventeen: All Roads 109

Chapter Eighteen: The Man Cave 115

Chapter Nineteen: Race! 121

Chapter Twenty: Boom! 125

Chapter Twenty One: A Hero is Born 129

Epilogue: Show's Not Over 134

Notes 141

Quotes 143

Boats 147

Reading Group Discussion Points 149

Women on Top 2
The Testicles

Three testaments on the life of Dud Wimpole by those who are said to have known Him

Written in the famed EB Garamond font.

INTRODUCTION

by Professor George C Cleftbottom

The ending of this book in which everybody dies horribly is a fitting conclusion to a sombre tale. At least, that is what I assume the ending to be. I have been very busy with marking, this week, and so have yet to finish the book, in a literal sense.

I did, though, read beyond the mid-section, comprising those sections of the book in which the seminal character Commandress Roseanne is introduced.

CR, through her initials, evokes Christ (the) Redeemer, in name and importance in the literary world of the novel. Her initials also allude, with simplistic obviousness, to that other mighty CR of our collective psyches, the Colorado Rapids (the geographic stretch of river and almost definitely not the US football team). It is clearly the intention of the authors, here, to bring to the fore the connotations of nature and power associated with that mighty passage of water. The third and final incantation in the ingenious use of that curious marriage of the letters CR, is, of course, the reference to the children's author, Chris Riddle. The meaning here is so clear it almost bears no need to state, for are not the initials of this complex character themselves an invitation to follow the White Rabbit down an endless hole of meaning and curiosity, resting finally, in the novel's true meaning, as a figurative parable commenting on the history of the Asian Silk Trade in the first decade of its maturity?

The elder Chief Commandress, meanwhile, is a classic quasi-subliminal-matriarchal figure in the tradition of Leviathan or Moby

Dick. Indeed, the entire narrative of The Testicles may be read, like Melville's master work, as a quest for "Dick."

So too, I must confess, has my own life. As I sit here in the bell tower, looking down upon the young men of the campus, I ask myself how long it will be until the University finds me. Not long, probably, if I keep banging my head on the bell whenever I get up out of bed.

Was my indiscretion deserving of such a hostile and immediate casting out? What was meant by the phrase "profligate with ejaculate," in the manifesto written against me by the Dean - the only thing the Dean has written, or had read, in the past decade I may add?

Was it so wrong, I ask, to spike a young man's drink with Rohypnol on a campus in which most of the students are drugged to the eyeballs anyway?

Enough of the legalities. So, to "The Testicles." Ah, yes, those mighty testicles. I draw, if I may, your attention to the pivotal Chapter 5 and the sentence upon which it opens, "We arrived at night." This is abruptly followed by, "I brought the ship to a halt on the moonlit ocean, a safe quarter mile outside the cliffs of the mainland." Thus follows, closing the paragraph, "With the ship hovering, gently, a few feet above water, we stood on the deck, Dud and I, in silence, contemplating the task at hand." There it is, in all its splendour. It can be gleaned from this, that Dud, and our speaker, have arrived at the mainland on a ship, and that the author almost certainly has a limp.

I haven't read the book.

I haven't read it, at all.

Professor George C Cleftbottom
24G Rutherford College
University of Kent

"Feminism is not just about women; it's about letting all people lead fuller lives." – Jane Fonda

PART ONE

PEARLS

A Testament by Cargo

CHAPTER ONE

SOMEONE WITH NOTHING

When I first met Dud Wimpole, he had nothing:
No home, no job, no family…
No title, no status, no money…
No cares, no plans, no responsibilities.
He had no orders, no commands, no obligations…
No stress, no anxiety, no pain…
No horror, no hell, no humiliations…
No moustache.
No nothing.
He was the happiest man alive.
Of course, all of that was about to change.

*

Dud Wimpole is the kind of guy you either love or hate.
As for me, well, I had some sympathy for the guy.
Hey, maybe I should be saying: Dud Wimpole is the kind
of guy you either love or hate, or have some sympathy for.
I could see how people got irritated by him.

Dud Wimpole is the kind of guy you either love or hate, or have some sympathy for, or who irritates the hell out of you.

When I met him he was living alone on an island.

You could see how a guy like this could get into trouble.

It started when I got the request to deliver what used to be called a Stanley Knife to some remote island in what used to be called the Pacific Ocean.

I say "what used to be called the Pacific Ocean," because when they, the ladies, found out that the ocean had been named by a man, they had to rename it. Now, it's called Lucy.

You could hear Dud's constant whistling as you approached that island from a mile away.

I delivered what was now called a Shirley Knife to that island in the middle of Lucy, and that's how I came to know Dud Wimpole.

Dud had decided to spend the rest of his life living off coconuts. He needed something to use to carve open the shells.

It wasn't a bad idea. The island was a five metres by five metres patch of sand with just two trees, one of which was dead. The other tree - that was still good - that still produced coconuts.

Dud ended up cutting himself with the knife trying to open a coconut, so next time round, he asked me to just bring him a carton of coconut milk. It turned out that cartoned milk gave Dud heartburn, so we ended up settling for condensed milk.

I'd have fished, myself, but Dud didn't seem like much of a fisherman. He didn't seem like much of anything, at first look, but looks can be deceiving.

See, when I met him, Dud Wimpole had managed to escape from the most dangerous place on the planet if you were unfortunate enough to have been born a guy - Dileag.

Hell, it's the one place on the planet I won't even go to.

Look at my business card. It says:

Cargo
Delivers stuff - anywhere
But not to Dileag

That's right, Dud Wimpole had not just survived Dileag; he had escaped Dileag, which makes him a person of interest in my book, and so I made an effort to get to know him.

I remember this one time, Dud and I are sitting on the sand, looking out at the ocean.

I'd delivered the usual haul of condensed milk, plus Dud's monthly order of glasses wipes, glasses tape, glasses nose-pad replacements… glasses stuff, basically.

This time round, I'd also outdone myself. I brought along a piece of fabric and showed Dud how to tie it between the two trees so it could be used as a hammock.

Dud struggled to climb into the thing without getting tangled up, spun round and thrown out, but he said he'd work on it.

I also brought along a couple of beers, snacks and some bottled water along with new batteries for the transmitter Dud used to contact me.

You see, I could tell that Dud was lonely. I could read the signs. He'd always shake my hand enthusiastically when I arrived, barely giving me the time to dock my ship off shore, allowing it to hover a few feet above the sea, and hop onto the sand. He'd always look a little sad when I left. He'd always ask how my day was. Plus, the guy lived on an island, so you put two and two together…

The ocean was calm and still. You could see how a person might get lost in their thoughts looking out to it. It reflected a person's face right back at them as sharp as a mirror.

Dud was struggling to open a beer can so I handed him a bottle of water instead.

The water was infused with lemon and made Dud wince.

It was enough to shake Dud from his internal reminiscing and start to talk.

Dud had been troubled in the night by an increasingly recurring nightmare - a flashback to his past.

"They made us line up in a cow shed and provide sperm samples into buckets," Dud says to me. "That was their way of telling which of us were Studs and which of us were Duds. You'd think they could just ask politely."

You see, Dileag was hit pretty hard from the fall out of the nuclear wars. They had a serious problem with infertility after that, and population growth. So when the ladies came to power, and faced with having to rebuild the world, they took it upon themselves to divide men between those who were fertile - the Studs - and those who were not - the Duds.

"How could they have thought I was a Stud?"

Dud had a point.

"There was some mix-up with one of the other testees in the shed. Stud Ramrod. He got sent off to enjoy sweeping nuclear waste all day, while I had to face the indignity of trying to impregnate the behemoth Commandress Roseanne."

I admit, now, it did occur to me that the guy may have been a loon.

I mean, how could a guy like this survive in Dileag? The place was famous for its hatred for males and, perhaps contradictorily, anything they saw to be "male inadequacy."

And not only how did he survive - how did he make it out of there?

I'd always told myself to believe the most likely scenario: either this guy was the only male in history to survive and escape that man-hating hell hole in one piece, or he was a loon. I admit, at that point in time, I was still entertaining the notion that he was most likely a loon.

"And when I failed to impregnate Commandress Roseanne, they hooked me up with her limo driver, Nicolette, a former gymnast in the hope that I would somehow impregnate her! I passed out! It was a colossal failure in a life filled with embarrassments, interspersed only by excruciating humiliation," Dud continued in his usual inspirational fashion.

"And then the real Stud Ramrod turned up. Meanwhile, I'd got involved in some war between Dileag and the Amazons over who was prettiest! I stole a hover ship and crash landed here, and I thought that would be the end of it. But the nightmares, they keep coming. I'm suffering from cold sweats - and we're in the tropics!"

Definite loon.

*

Loon, though he may be, there was something about Dud Wimpole that made me want to help him.

Maybe it was the helplessness of the guy, stuck there on that island, in the middle of Lucy. Maybe it was his story about escaping Dileag, escaping the ladies, which, even if it wasn't true, makes a guy think.

He had the distant, haunted look of a man whose life had been dominated by women.

And yet, here he was, apparently free. That had to account for something.

Maybe there was something in me that made me want to save the guy.

Or maybe it was because, even then, something deep down told me that he was the guy who was going to save us all.

Although that wasn't always obvious, looking at him there, in his blue swimming shorts, and his ragged t-shirt with some kind of logo with a faded ghost on it. Maybe that's what he wanted to be. A ghost.

Maybe that's not such a bad thing to be.

"Why couldn't they have left me alone?" Dud says, seemingly talking to himself, now, lost in his own memories.

"Dud, I better be going," I tell the little guy.

Dud springs to his feet.

"Sure, sure. No problem. Thanks for the stuff, Cargo."

That's what they call me. Cargo. Because I deliver cargo. Since the ladies had taken over pretty much every country on the planet, those ladies decided that men should be stripped of their names. That's the one thing they seemed to agree on. Now we're usually just referred to in terms of whatever function we perform.

To tell the truth, I didn't have a problem with it. Who needs a name? As for the whole women on top thing, it didn't bother me too much. My own mother was probably a woman, so what issue did I have if the ladies ruled the world? It was just the way things were.

This guy, though. I could see it being a problem for this guy, especially in a place like Dileag where not only are you hated for being a man, after all the problems men caused by bringing about an apocalypse and all, but also where a guy's whole purpose is to get a lady pregnant...

So, Dud reaches into his pocket and pulls out a pearl. My payment. It's a beauty.

And then I remember.

"There's this one more thing," I tell the guy, and I hand him a letter I'd picked up at the depot.

"A letter for me?" Dud asks, turning the thing over, not quite believing. "That's impossible."

But there's his name on the front: Dud Wimpole. Addressed to: "Wherever the little shit may be."

And on the back, a return address: Dileag.

This seems to affect Dud Wimpole on some level, because he lets out a heroic, high-pitch scream, scurries over to one of the trees and starts to dig a hole in the sand. Those are some of the signs that a guy has been affected by something.

Looking at Dud Wimpole like that, scurrying in the sand on all fours, trying to bury that letter, his ass sticking up at the sky, you really wouldn't think that this guy would turn out to be an all time legend, a leader of men, a hero of heroes.

No way.

But there 'ain't no doubting it - that's exactly who Dud Wimpole turned out to be.

16

CHAPTER TWO

ENOUGH ABOUT ME

I guess I should tell you a bit more about myself. They call me Cargo. You know that. I deliver stuff. It suits me. I deliver anywhere, except to Dileag. But you know that, too. What else is there?

The stuff I deliver? Well, mostly I deliver:
Clothing
Cosmetics
Shoes
Shampoos
Sanitary pads
Nail gloss
Hand cream
Trinkets
Hand-bags
Compact mirrors
Chocolates
Sweets
Wine
Champagne

Gin
Tonic water
Mobile phones
Perfumes
Most of what I deliver are gifts for ladies or stuff ladies want or machinery to produce stuff ladies want.

It seems like they need a lot of stuff but who am I to question? I just deliver the stuff and it suits me fine.

I find that spending all my time alone on a cargo ship is a perfectly healthy way to live.

I'd describe myself as a lover of music. Sometimes, when I transport musical instruments, I'll unpack them and lay them out at the stern of the ship as though it's a stage and since I can't play one, I'll just stand among them with my eyes closed and imagine I'm in a rock band.

Aside from that, to entertain myself, I mostly enjoy humping stuff.

It gets lonely sometimes, delivering cargo, but that's ok... I find that humping stuff relieves a lot of tension.

I started mostly humping pillows but there ain't many pillows on a cargo ship, so I moved on to stuff that had holes, like:
Canisters
Trash shoots
Turbine parts
Flasks
Exhaust fixings
Tyres
Inner tubes
Chair necks
Hat racks
Coiled rope
Small boxes

And then I moved on to stuff that didn't have holes, like:
Display screens
Windows
Doors
Panelling
The floor
Walls
The stove
Large boxes
But hey, that's enough about me.

*

The way Dud Wimpole reacted to receiving that letter got me thinking. So, while I was away on my travels, I made some enquiries on the guy. When you do that, you start to hear certain things.

The word was - and this in no way can be verified - and I can't tell you where I heard it from, because they're long gone, anyway. But the word was, Dud didn't just escape Dileag, he created a kind of uprising which almost levelled the place.

That's what I hear.

The details are fuzzy, but apparently some Studs were involved, as well as the menfolk of a powerful Commandress. Apparently they stole some planes and dropped some good old fashioned TNT onto Dileag before crashing out in a blaze of glory. That's what caused the distraction for Dud to escape.

You don't hear it in public, because if it's true, it stands as a major blow to the lady leaders of Dileag, and since they control the news anyway, they won't be wanting something like that leaking out.

But that ain't all. It turns out that since then, the ladies have employed the children of Dileag to pretty much rebuild the city. How good a job they're doing is anyone's guess. Since the bombing, pretty much nobody goes in, and nobody goes out.

There are some things though, it seems, that can't be kept down, that can't be stopped.

Like the truth.

And Dud Wimpole.

*

Dud asked me something once that stuck with me.

He asked me what I thought of when I thought about freedom.

Truth is, when I think about freedom, I think about my father.

As for myself, I've never been without it - freedom. The kind of work I'm in, you go from A to B on your own schedule, nobody telling you what to do, nobody to answer to. My father was a cargo guy, too, so maybe it's in the blood.

But before that, before he was a cargo guy, my father was an insurance agent, and it's possible that he was the unhappiest guy in the world.

When the nuclear war came, he was happy about it! While everyone else was desperately trying to find a bunker, or sewer, or subway station in which they could hide, Dad took to the streets in celebration, his arms held up wide, screaming "Our premiums don't cover this."

Despite being a kid, it was up to me to pull Dad into a subway station and save his life. Mom was away at a three-month Mindfulness retreat and the way Dad told it, a nuclear bomb probably landed on her head.

After the bombs had settled, and people emerged from the rubble, Dad had the foresight to take ownership of an old cargo ship. It was the kind of ugly work the new women leaders of the world were not interested in taking, and it gave Dad a living.

As for Dud Wimpole, though, he'd say strange things like, "Maybe freedom is having no purpose, or nothing to live for," and crazy stuff like that, which I never understood, until the next time I saw him after delivering that letter.

He was standing on the shore waiting for me.

He looked as white as the ghost on his t-shirt.

In his hand, he held the letter.

It was open.

Dud was not in a good way. Here was a guy tormented by his past, trying to escape a profound and bone-chilling trauma. Plus a tsunami hit the island overnight and washed away all his condensed milk.

"Cargo," he says to me. "I want you to take me back to Dileag."

CHAPTER THREE

WHAT MAKES A DUD?

"Cargo, I'm ready to leave," Dud kept saying, as though in a trance. "I have to go back."

You know, some of the old societies used to punish the harshest crimes by taking away the perpetrator's liberty? Why, then, would any man, under any circumstances, willingly give up his freedom?

What would that make him?

I kept asking myself, what kinda asshole goes back to the place he spent his life trying to escape?

And I may have said it out loud because Dud seemed to hear my thoughts.

"If I don't go back I'll live with guilt for the rest of my life," he says. "Please don't call me an asshole."

Now, here's what I know about Dud Wimpole. And here's why him asking me to take him back to Dileag was, not just out of character, but borderline nuts.

Dud Wimpole is a harm avoider. He told me that his island home was the perfect home for him because nobody or nothing could hurt him there. He was particularly fond of the sand because it was soft and, he said proudly, it didn't chafe his feet.

Dud Wimpole is a tiny little guy. What's more, he had the frail, slight build of someone who'd spent the majority of his life in an office cubicle, and his recent years reclining on the super soft sand of an island in the middle of Lucy. The stature of the man gave nothing to suggest that he was equipped to lead a one man war against the dominant world order.

Dud Wimpole is a loner. There was something about being on the island that suited the guy. When I brought him a wind-up gramophone I found on the black market, he asked me to only bring him instrumental music because the sound of voices singing gave him headaches.

Dud Wimpole is intensely disappointing to women. He'd got fired from his first job - in the Ministry of Sending Endless Compliments to Females, because the most imaginative thing he could come up with in a whatsapp message was, "You have a full set of teeth and many hair follicles."

He was a self confessed failure as a Stud, both infertile and, as a result of being raised in a lady led society, impotent. Plus, he had the habit of whistling both when he was happy, and when he was nervous, which was unnerving, and irritated the hell out of any lady who heard.

But, he persisted.

"I have to go back to Dileag," he kept saying.

He wouldn't tell me what was in the letter or why he was going back to Dileag because, he said, I'd try to talk him out of it.

Damn right, I would.

*

One final thing I'll tell you about the nature of the guy.

One time, I was delivering Dud's monthly supplies to the island and I caught him half way up one of the trees - the one which still bore coconuts.

This was still in the early days of Dud's time on the island, when he was still entertaining the notion of living off coconuts; so I see him there and I assume he's making the climb to try to get to the fruit.

Turns out, though, that a baby bird had fallen out of the tree, and that I'd caught Dud in the middle of a rescue mission.

"Look, Cargo, look," Dud says, and he pulls open a pocket in his blue swim shorts to reveal this little baby bird peeking out. "It fell from its nest!"

Luckily enough, I have sharp metal spikes in the ship yet to be delivered, a popular weapon for wives in the Eastern Seaboard, so I gather an arm full of those and bring them over to the tree.

That makes climbing much easier, and together, Dud and I climb that coconut tree to the top, with that baby bird nestled safely in Dud's pocket.

It's giddy at the top. A person could get vertigo up that high. But we focus on the task at hand. There's the bird nest from which the baby bird had fallen. There's the mother bird, surrounded by a batch of unhatched eggs.

With me holding on to Dud to provide support, Dud gently takes the baby bird from his shorts pocket, cradling the little thing in his hands. He slowly, ever so carefully, places the baby bird back in the nest, and both Dud and I sigh in satisfaction at our good work.

Then, you know what?

That mother bird takes one look at that baby bird, and she swallows the baby bird whole.

Then she flies off squawking like a maniac.

*

Dud let out a "Woohoo!" as the ship did a 180 and I flew the thing away from the island.

He'd risked everything to escape Dileag. He'd risked his life. He'd achieved the impossible. And here he was heading straight back into the lion's den, the wind blowing through his hair like he was some puppy with his head out the car window.

This asshole really doesn't seem like the future saviour of mankind, I thought to myself.

"I don't know what you're talking about," Dud says. "And stop calling me an asshole."

"We got two stops ahead," I point out. "Major islands. First is Beyonce 1. That's where we pick up some fuel for this thing."

"Right!" Dud shouts into the wind.

"Next is the island formerly known as Solange. Now, Beyonce 2. They got a great burger place. We gotta get some fuel for ourselves before we face Dileag."

"Great," says Dud. "I could eat a horse! Not literally, of course. Meat products give me gas," he continues stoically. "I can handle vegetarian burgers, unless they're curried - for obvious reasons!"

See what I mean?

Really irritating guy.

CHAPTER FOUR

THE BEYONCE ISLANDS

"Why do you have so many tractor magazines stashed around the ship?" Dud asks as we approached the Beyonce islands. "And why do you collect machine parts - canisters, exhaust pipes, metal tubing?"

"There's Beyonce 1!"

I point out the silhouette of three perfectly triangular mountains appearing on the horizon.

With our destination in sight, I accelerate the ship forward. Dud holds onto the railing so as not to be thrown backwards. That puts a stop to the questioning. I can tell he was about to ask why I had posters around the ship of turbines being hosed down with water, and to tell the truth, I don't have an answer.

As we approach the island, the mountains of Beyonce 1 become clearer to view. Now, I've been around, I've seen some things, but even for me, Beyonce 1's mountains are a sight to behold.

"What the?" Dud starts again with the questioning.

You see, the mountains of Beyonce 1 are no ordinary

mountains. Each is, in fact, a sky-high pile of accessories. The first is a pile of shoes. The second is a pile of lipsticks. The third is a pile of handbags.

I draw the ship nearer to handbag mountain, a monument to designer junk, and begin to fly the vessel towards the summit.

"First they filled their homes, then they filled their cities, then they filled their rubbish dumps. Now they have these mountains. There's nowhere else to put all this stuff."

"Why do they do it?" Dud asks, still with the questions.

"That's just the way it is here. The women consume, the men work so that the women can consume, never ending, no break, on and on."

At the top of handbag mountain, figures come into view: bent, crippled figures, dragging their legs up the slope, each with one hand desperately fixed against their foreheads.

"What are they - zombies?" Dud asks.

"No," I explain. "Those are the men."

I station the ship on auto-hover a few feet above the summit. Dud and I lean over the railings on deck.

Below us, it isn't a pretty sight. A group of gaunt figures reach up to the ship with their single free hands. They wear an arrangement of straps around their thighs, to accentuate the testicles, and they moan:

"Uuuurgh."

"We need fuel." I call out. "We bring you ten kilos of authentic designer merchandise."

"Uuuuuurgh…" the tragic bastards moan back.

"We haven't got all day!"

You've gotta be firm.

So I release a pulley, which drops an empty life-boat platform onto the pile of handbags, and figures load the fuel onto the platform. They know the routine. Dud watches all of this with a mix of horror and sadness.

"Your women will be very happy," I call out. "This is some top-of-the-range, classic designer junk."

I pull another lever and that releases a door beneath the hull of the ship. Ten kilos of handbags drop onto the mountain and the figures fall to their knees in grateful worship. It isn't a nice thing to see.

Dud turns his head away from the sight below. He's seen enough, and an old Louis Vuitton handbag narrowly misses his face, thrown onto the ship by one of the figures below, seemingly out of spite.

I steer the ship away from Beyonce 1.

"They seemed nice," Dud says, trying to lighten the mood.

"Hold tight. We need some fuel, too."

And I set course for Beyonce 2, already drooling at the thought of double whoppers.

*

The first thing you hear when you approach Beyonce 2 is the clicking. That's the sound of high-heels, permanently nailed into the feet of the island's menfolk - an act of revenge against the unreasonable beauty standards imposed on ladies in olden times.

Beyonce 2 itself is little more than a concrete pit-stop, with a self-service garage, a convenience store and a 24 hour burger joint, but hey, it's the only place you can pick up something to eat before making the long trip to the mainland.

It was to the burger joint that we were headed, now. I dock the ship in the parking lot alongside fellow planetary delivery vehicles, and Dud and I head inside. The door is held open for us by a polite old gent who is still bleeding from the heels.

I steer Dud over to a booth in the corner which already has a couple of menus on the table: Beyonce 2 Burger, Beyonce 2 BBQ Burger, Beyonce 2 Bacon Burger.

"They sure like their burgers," Dud observes, shouting over an old song about single ladies needing rings on their fingers or something that was blaring from speakers overhead.

"As long as we just focus on our food and don't engage, we'll be fine," I warn my awkward companion. "The women here get very upset if they sense a man is thinking about them in a sexual way."

"Right," says Dud, and then he immediately does exactly what you don't want to do on Beyonce 2. He starts looking around the place.

The waitresses in the joint are all dressed in highly provocative clothing - red bikinis, lingerie and rubber. Each is wearing a name-badge. Some carry whips.

"Right," Dud repeats to himself.

I should have known, right then and there, that we were in trouble. I should have just pulled Dud from his seat and got the hell out of the place, but it was already too late. A voluptuous young waitress in tight red spandex swans over to our table

"What are you guys hungry for?" the waitress asks as she leans over our table to adjust some forks and knives in the holder.

I try to bury my face in the menu, and I tell her:

"Burgers, we'll have the burgers, right Dud?"

Before he can answer, the waitress interrupts with:

"Get me out of here!"

"Excuse me?" I ask.

"I can't work here, forever. There must be something I can do for you?" she says.

"Ah, does that come with fries?"

I'm trying to defuse the situation.

Meanwhile, Dud is blinking like crazy behind his horn rimmed glasses across the table.

"At least pay for my college," the waitress continues, reaching into her chest, pulling out a nipple ring, and throwing it on the table. "Here, you can take this. Just pay for my Master's."

Then Dud gets involved:

"I'd be very happy with a veggie burger," he says. "It would make a nice change from condensed milk"

"What's that supposed to mean?" asks the waitress.

"Nothing," I tell her, trying to rescue the situation.

"Why's he looking at me like that, with his beady little eyes?" the waitress asks, immediately irritated by the guy.

"He isn't looking at you like that," I say to her.

"Oh, so I'm not attractive enough for you?" she asks.

And so Dud says:

"You're very attractive…"

Here's what happens. The waitress stands erect. Her face drops.

"What did he say?" she asks me.

The place goes silent.

Dud starts whistling nervously.

And the waitress starts screaming:

"Pervert! We've got ourselves a pervert!"

An alarm goes off. Lights start to flash.

Angry, bikini-clad staff surround the table.

The knee-high rubber booted, lingerie wearing manageress takes the lead.

She screams:

"Bring forth the branding iron, for this pervert!"

The chef brings out an iron bar with the letter P red hot at one end.

And then Dud does something I'll never forget.

He brings out a pearl from his little blue shorts pocket, holds it up, and declares:

"Wait, ladies. This is for you!"

Then he pretends to fumble it, so the pearl falls and rolls over to the far corner of the joint. Talk about quick thinking!

The waitresses scramble over each other to try to catch the pearl, pulling at each other's hair, biting each other's arms. The manageress leaps onto the pile of women and starts scratching at their eyes.

Lunch is over

*

Dud and I burst out of the burger joint, pushing through a crowd of men in high heels, toppling the hopeless bastards over into a heap on the tarmac.

An electronic billboard stationed over the parking lot flashes the word "Perverts" over profile pictures of myself and Dud, seemingly taken at the booth moments before, particularly wide-eyed and unflattering, along with the slogan underneath: #youtoo.

We had to get out of there, fast!

We climb into the ship with the alarm now sounding out across the island.

"Hold on!" I tell Dud.

Dud throws his arms around me.

"Not to me," I tell him.

Dud grabs the railing.

The hover engines kick in and within seconds I careen the ship off the parking lot, smashing through the exit barriers and heading off and away from Beyonce 2.

Not for the first time that day, Dud Wimpole surprises me. He pulls out two burgers from under his t-shirt.

"That was smart," I tell him.
"I'll have the salad," Dud says.
And then we flew to Dileag.

CHAPTER FIVE

DILEAG

We arrived at night.

I brought the ship to a halt on the moonlit ocean, a safe quarter mile outside the cliffs of the mainland. With the ship hovering, gently, a few feet above water, we stood on the deck, Dud and I, in silence, contemplating the task at hand.

First thing I did when I inherited the ship, after Dad was executed for exposing his smile to a lady on Beyonce 2, was install the hover conversion.

This meant I could go wherever I liked, be wherever I liked.

One place I never did go, was Dileag

Until now.

Picture it:

It's silent.

In the distance, a spotlight runs across the cliff face, monoliths rising out of the sea. No one goes in, no one goes out.

The spotlight swings its attention to the ship and Dud flinches.

"It's ok, we have freight clearance. We better get started," I tell him.

I perform one final check on the stack of crates I've got ready for delivery.

"You'll climb inside one of these. They'll be sending a transport vessel right about now to pick these up. Then you'll feel yourself being lifted up the cliff face by a crane. It's the only way to get onto land."

"It's all Viagra," Dud observes, reading the freight labels.

Each crate is stickered up with labels: "Viagra, Viagra, Viagra," slogans: "Viagra: you'll need it," and medical guidance: "Don't take if you're over 120 years old - unless she orders you to."

"Dileag is the largest importer of Viagra in the world. I can't imagine why... Are you sure you don't want to turn back?" I ask the little guy.

Dud gulps:

"When I'm over the city walls, how do I find Commandress Roseanne?"

*

Dud stands over a holographic 3D map of Dileag, projected from the ship's control panel.

"This is only a predicted layout, taken from satellite images. They don't allow cartographers into the city, because they think cartographers are nerds"

"Of course," Dud says.

The map suggests there's a kilometre or so from the cliff top to the city walls.

"A freight truck will pick you up from the cliff top. That'll take you to the city. It's the only way to get through the city walls."

"Do you have any travel sickness pills?" Dud asks.

Ignoring this, I continue:

"The freight is dropped in a warehouse right on the other side of the wall, at the edge of the city. That's where you make your escape."

I hand Dud a Shirley Knife.

"So you can get yourself out of the crate. Don't cut yourself," I tell him.

He and I try to make sense of the map.

"Looks like this is the first landmark to aim for - a stadium," I tell him.

"I know it," Dud says.

"And from there, through the city centre, or what's left of it."

The holographic images depict what seem to be monuments to the female form, huge architectural domes with nipple appendages at the top. Some have been damaged, others are half rubble. A number have been rebuilt, as though by a child playing with building blocks - huge, incoherent squares.

"They got the children to rebuild the city," Dud figures.

"It's cheap labour."

The centre of the city is dominated by a massive structure.

"That's the mall," Dud observes. "They've expanded it. Commandress Roseanne's mansion is on the other side of the city. I can make it by foot."

"You'll be arriving early morning, so you have a chance of getting there undetected, but Dud…" and this has been playing on my mind. "What makes you think she's going to welcome you back with open arms?"

"I expect she'll have taken my escape as a personal rejection. She'll prioritise her ego above all else. There'll be some healing to do before she can get round to the business of executing me for subversion.”

“Are you sure?”

“I’m banking on it.”

*

“Are you absolutely certain you want to do this?”

“If I don’t, I’ll never forgive myself,” Dud says, reaching into those bottomless pockets of his. He pulls out a fake moustache and sticks it on his face. “Studs are free to move around, usually on errands. They all have moustaches. Any Dud spotted walking around is likely to be shot on the spot.”

I look at him there, with his horn-rimmed glasses and his oversized moustache, an expression of desperate hope on his face, and I have this terrible sinking feeling in the pit of my stomach.

We hear the sound of the transport vessel approaching.

I hold open one of the crate boxes for Dud and he climbs in, nestling into a pile of Viagra.

“Cargo,” he says to me. “Thank you, for everything. You’ve been a good friend to me.”

“Don’t mention it,” I tell him. “Besides, I’m doing it for all of us. I have a feeling you’ll save us all.”

I close him in.

As I watched Dud go, inside one of those crates, across the last stretch of ocean towards the mainland, and then lifted up the side of that cliff-face, I couldn’t help but feel a little responsible, you know?

Although I had a feeling he would save us all, how was Dud Wimpole going to save himself? That I couldn’t see happening. Maybe I should have told him that before sticking him in a box.

"I have a feeling you'll save us all."
Those were the last words I ever said to Dud Wimpole.

CHAPTER SIX

APPENDIX TO PART ONE: TIMELINE - BY CARGO

So, here's what I figure about the timings of all this, based on my estimates, personal experiences, word on the street and conversations with Dud Wimpole.

Year One (Around 2040 in the old calendar):

Frustrated by what they see as the increasing feminisation of the planet, the men of the world respond with violence, unleashing a mad and indiscriminate nuclear strike on pre-programmed targets, including what used to be East Coast USA. Myself, five years old at the time, and my father take to the subways. The male who would become Dud Wimpole is born in a fallout shelter.

Year Two:

People emerge from the underground. It becomes apparent that women now outnumber men 10 to 1, the evacuation to the underground having been operated under a women and children first policy. Women across the world decide that men are unfit to rule, and in locations across the planet form new societies based on new female led orders.

Year Three:

Dileag is formally named and emerges as a leading female led society, based on commerce. Dad's cargo business flourishes. Rumours of fertility issues caused by the nuclear fallout begin to circulate.

Year Twenty Two:

Dileag, amongst many societies, acknowledges that its fertility issue will lead to population extinction unless addressed. The Commandresses, the ruling class in the society, implement a plan. Men will be divided into Studs, those who are fertile - assigned to impregnate Commandresses, and Duds, those who are infertile - assigned to sweep nuclear waste. The programme begins slowly, under the shroud of secrecy.

Year Thirty Two:

The largest batch yet of Dileag's "free men" is rounded up and assigned to the fertility programme. Among them is he who would become known as Dud Wimpole. He is mistaken to be Stud Ramrod and is assigned to impregnate Commandress Roseanne. Stud Ramrod is assigned to clean nuclear waste. My father is executed for smiling at a waitress in Beyonce 2, and I take over the cargo business, adding a hover conversion to the ship.

The Wimpole-Ramrod mix up is uncovered. Ramrod appears at the household of Commandress Roseanne. Dud Wimpole escapes Dileag. A small uprising of disgruntled Studs bomb Dileag using old TNT explosives and disguarded war planes. The incident is covered up by Dileag, which becomes increasingly insular.

Year Thirty Three:

I begin delivering to Dud Wimpole on a remote island in Lucy.

Year Thirty Four:

Dud Wimpole returns to Dileag.

PART TWO

WALNUTS

A Testament by Commandress Roseanne

CHAPTER SEVEN

I AM ALWAYS READY

Our time together is about to begin, dear reader. Possibly you will view these pages of mine as a fragile treasure box, to be opened with the utmost care. Possibly you will tear them apart, or eat them, for indeed you may be a wild and untamed beast.

Yes, oh yes, that is probably what will happen.

Only dead people are allowed to have statues, but I have had one created of myself while still alive. It was unveiled in my garden.

I pulled the rope that released the drape cloth shrouding me; it billowed to the ground and there I stood. The men of the household are not permitted to cheer, but there was some discreet clapping.

I then pulled the rope that released the drape cloth shrouding the statue of me; it also billowed to the ground and there we stood: the statue and I, facing each other, naked.

There was no clapping this time. The men were in awe. We did this at night so as not to alarm the neighbours.

My statue is larger than life, as statues tend to be, and

shows me as younger, slimmer by half, approximating the mere 100kg I carried as a young woman.

The lips are curved into a firm but benevolent pout, and so are the lips on the face. Long deceased, the sculptor has followed instructions meticulously, but he will never testify to this, because his head has fallen off with old age.

At least I look sane.

*

I write these words in the private sanctum of the corner library of my living room - one of the few libraries remaining after the enthusiastic book burnings we have ordered across the land.

The violent and blood-smeared fingerprints of the past must be wiped away to create a clean space for the morally pure generation that we are trying to conceive.

If you are reading, this manuscript will at least have survived. Though, perhaps I am fantasising; perhaps I will never have a reader. Perhaps I'll only be talking to the walls, in more ways than one.

These walls are filled with remnants of the past: artefacts. Weapons from across the ages hang from wall to wall, crossbows, swords, rifles. They give me comfort.

Among them, stuffed and mounted, is my former house husband. His name was It. He serves more use to me now than he did when alive, arriving, as he did, as a promotion when I bought the sofa.

He is elevated from having been part of the furniture to the role of posthumous trophy husband. Literally. He would have wanted it that way.

He provides companionship while I write, while I wait - while I wait for the return of Dud Wimpole.

*

I hear you ask, how can I be certain that the Dud we labelled Wimpole will return?

Allow me to enlighten you, my reader.

Dud Wimpole will return because I am Commadress Roseanne, and I am the sexiest dancer in Dileag.

Dud Wimpole will return because I am a stable, intelligent, arousing, interesting, desirable and delectable delight.

Dud Wimpole will return because he is in love with me.

Yes, I sent Dud Wimpole a letter, pretending to be from my former driver Nicolette, and claiming that she had birthed a child of Wimpole himself.

The child, of course, was fathered by someone else, the Stud known as Ramrod. Dud Wimpole is as fertile as a squashed worm. Dud Wimpole knows this himself! However, these are mere superficialities.

The letter was merely a prompt, a nudge, to permit Dud Wimpole to return to me, as he so desired, without confronting the glare of reality. His delusion and desire would do the rest.

That reality, dear reader, so painful to the male ego, is that a man is nothing without a female to serve, and having served the mightiest of all Commandresses, there was only one place Dud Wimpole could go...

Crawling right back into the enchanting clutch of my crevice.

50

CHAPTER EIGHT

I KNOW HOW TO CONTROL A MAN

It was a cold and wind swept morning the day Dud Wimpole returned to Dileag. I was at home stroking my hairy pussy - a Persian - stuffed, when I heard the knock upon my door.

I knew the precise time he would arrive, of course, right down to the second, for I had him tracked. Cameras followed his movements as he entered the city walls, darting surreptitiously from corner to crook, crouching down behind parked cars, flattening himself against alleyways, peering round corners, believing himself to be beyond detection because he was wearing a big fake moustache.

At the sound of the feeble knocks upon the door, I collected Nicolette's brat from the crib to which he was chained and strode to face my suitor.

I opened the door.

At once, the eyes of Dud Wimpole fell upon the child. I had arranged for the creature to be attired exactly as Wimpole appeared on those trusted CCTV images: blue shorts, black shirt, thick horn-rimmed glasses frames, enough to complete the conviction in the Dud's mind that the child was his, a conviction he so desperately desired.

The ruse was complete. Dud looked to the child with an expression of instantaneous awe, wonder and love.

"I knew you'd come back for me," I told the scrawny bastard.

*

When face to face with a man, either for the first time or after a period of absence, it is essential, my reader, to establish dominance. Allow me to explain how.

Firstly, fix the man with a firm, unblinking stare. Secondly, affect a deep, baritone voice. Third, remain calm.

Dud Wimpole and I circled each other in my living room like two champion prize fighters returning to the ring for one epic, decisive bout. I stared at him, and I stared at him hard.

Dud, whether through nerves, or through delight at seeing me, began to whistle.

Wrong move!

I swung my hand and slapped him hard across the face, sending his glasses flying.

"I've slapped many men in my life and they've all deserved it!" I told him.

"Your eyes are twitching," were his first words to me.

"You think you can walk back in here like nothing happened?" I bellowed, sinking my jowls into my neck for added reverberation. "After running off like that in full view of my subjects, making me look ridiculous, when to lead, image is everything!"

"Flying off," Dud said, hunting for his glasses behind the sofa.

"Flying off. While your friends bombed our city, Stud Ramrod, Stud Mastall, Marku, Niko, even my house husband - It - hanging there, stuffed!"

Fourth, never feel ashamed to take a moment in order to recompose oneself.

That moment came for me as Dud flinched at the sight of It, my former house husband, stuffed and hung upon the wall, looking down on us with that same inane expression he'd worn throughout his life.

I took the opportunity to take a crossbow from the wall and playfully fire some darts in the direction of Dud Wimpole, three of which he ducked, two of which he leapt over and one of which became lodged in an antique designer bag he whipped from his shirt as a gift, a desperate and futile attempt to win me over and access my enchanted cave (I later used the bag two or three times and then threw it away in spite).

Fifth: set boundaries.

"Don't you think you're going to just walk back in here and have a piece of this!" I advised. "I hate you! You and your friends. You're a bunch of toxics."

"Toxins?" asked Dud, trying to catch his breath.

"Toxics! Don't try to change the words! That's what we call your kind, now."

To tell the truth, dear reader, although "toxics" had become the favoured nomenclature for the male kind, I still hold a soft spot for the word men. I find that it lends itself so delightfully well to being spoken with poisonous venom. Men. Men. Men. One can almost spit it out. Men. Still, in that moment, I calculated that showing off our new words would further disorientate Dud, (Six: disorientate the man), so I added:

"Are you going to start tox-plaining things to me, now, while tox-spreading your legs? We have many hateful words for your kind. A lot has changed since you've been away."

Refusing to delay the big reveal any further, I inched my dress up above my leg to expose the glorious addition to my shapely thigh: a tattoo depicting a penis with a dagger through it.

"Alluring," admitted Dud.

Seven: use sex.

"Don't think I trust you, Dud Wimpole, because I don't. You're going to have to prove you deserve a second chance. Prove that you're here for me."

"How old is he?" Dud asked cryptically.

"Who?"

Dud pointed to the child, still held under my arm.

"I don't know. He doesn't speak," I told the fool.

"What's his name?"

"He hasn't told me! He - doesn't - speak," (Eight: remember that men lack empathy and understanding). "He looks like a nerd, though. You're a nerd! You need to win me over. Earn my trust!"

"How about a walk in the park?" Dud proposed. "Somewhere with easy access to the city exits."

"Done!"

And that's what happens when you learn to handle yourself well.

*

Dud followed me to the front door, fawning over my grand presence.

I handed him a lime green tunic from the coat hanger. It had belonged to It, and was the designated uniform of Dileag house husbands. It would enable Dud to escort me freely in public without raising attention.

With it, came a white bonnet.

The bonnet would shroud Dud from the view of the public, a necessity since the squirt, as Stud Ramrod, had become somewhat recognisable in his latter days in Dileag.

Indeed, despite my magnanimous diplomacy, Dileag had been involved in a minor disagreement with the women of another society over who was the most deserving of male servitude (we are). To settle the affair, Dud had been offered as a combatant against the opponent's most fearsome warrior.

The fact that he managed to survive counted as a victory on our part, a victory overshadowed by the (other) fact that he promptly ran away while his friends bombed the city.

The bonnet suited him.

"Are we just going to leave him here?" Dud asked.

"Who?"

"The baby."

Something in me stirred.

I admit, now, that being abandoned by one's assigned Stud had affected me. Seeing him run off like that, fly off, while my city crumbled behind me, had made an impression on me that I had not cared to acknowledge.

These feelings, and so many more, were coming to the fore. I am, after all, despite my power, my poise and probably some other things I can't think of right now beginning with "p," I am also a sensitive, beautiful woman.

"You are here for me, aren't you?" I heard myself saying.

"Of course," said my transfixed suitor.

"Ok, but you can carry him."

I took the baby from the coat rack from which I had placed him and handed him to Dud, along with a strap-on baby carrier.

The door was opened for us by the ever reliable Chantelle. I introduced her to Dud.

"This is my new driver, Chantelle. She's also my PA and Head of Comms."

"Hello," said Dud.

"She can't talk, Dud," I explained. "Deaf, dumb and mute. Positive discrimination. Last thing you want when trying to lead a totalitarian feminist state is meritocracy."

"Ah," Dud nodded. I think he understood.

"She can't drive either. Here."

I handed Dud the keys to the car.

It was time for our date.

CHAPTER NINE

I HAVE MANY CHARMING QUIRKS

The park was bright and green and beautiful. A number of billboards, replacing scorched and unkept trees, displayed glowing adverts for the season's hot new items, casting a glowing ambience on the cobbled path.

Magnificently crafted marble fountains, shaped like vaginas, spewed water in all directions.

I dragged Dud Wimpole by the wrist, the smaller nerd strapped to his torso, as we enjoyed our sunny surroundings.

"How pleasant it is to walk in the park," I observed.

"It's very large. Where's the way out?" Dud mumbled.

I could tell he was nervous. A smattering of small talk was needed.

"As soon as Nicolette gave birth to your child, I had her slaughtered and then claimed the baby as my own," I began, the breeze delicately coursing through my luxuriant hair. "I'm not sure if her neck snapped in the hanging or if she suffocated, but either way it was a gruesome death. Lovely flowers."

Dud nodded in profound agreement.

"The baby helped me recover some of the status I'd lost with your disappearance, plus it satiated the spite I had for the mother for being thinner than me. There's a self-service hot-dog stand up there. Hungry?"

"Surprisingly not."

"You know in France, they've started eating cock-dogs? Gotta love the French. Quick, look at my phone."

"Why, what's wrong with it?" Dud asked.

I took a photo of the three of us: myself pouting seductively, Dud looking mystified, sweat dripping from his face, the baby with a finger up its nose. We were an unusual trio, but it just worked.

It wasn't easy for Dud Wimpole, all of this; that I understood. Yes, I had allowed his male ego to believe he had returned to protect Nicolette's child, and this was a psychological front to cover the obvious lure of my charms. But on a deeper, primal level, Dud Wimpole was irresistibly motivated by a need from which he would never escape - the need to satisfy me sexually.

Let me explain, my dear reader. Nothing impacts a male's brain quite so significantly as the man's own sexual performance. This performance, good or bad, can even have a physiological effect on the said brain, designed, as it is, with only one purpose - to figure out how to satisfy a woman's carnal urges.

Dud's extraordinary failure in our love making rituals had clearly made their marks on his organ (I'm still talking about his brain - my case in point).

Deep down, Dud knew that the only way to reverse the physiological damage he had inflicted upon himself by failing my loins, and to get his brain working at full capacity, was to sexually ravish me as I'd never been ravished before. But it wasn't going to be easy for Dud. I was going to play hard to get. I was going to tease him. I was going to make him work for his redemption.

My stomach let out a cute and delicate roar.

"Come, I'll let you feed me," I told my suitor, pulling him over to the hot-dog stand with a skip and a flourish, and feeling, for the first time in a very long time, truly alive.

*

It wasn't always like this, of course.

Under the old world order, a woman's life was spent avoiding the big O (oppression) and chasing the other big O (orgasms). I got plenty of the former and not so much of the latter.

Case in point: My first job out of college was as a tutor of French. The College Director, a man, fired me unexpectedly one day and when I asked him why, he said it was because I didn't know any French.

This was a story known all too well to many a young lady in those dark times, with women being passed up for roles they were as incapable of fulfilling as any man, getting paid less for jobs they may or may not have been qualified for and being unfairly treated by men who couldn't handle their strength.

I gave that College Director the finger and said to him, "Adios." I think I'd made my point.

I took an online course on the male mind while touring India to find myself. The tour was worthwhile, as it turned out I wasn't actually in India. I passed the course with flying colours and was presented with a certificate - also in colour.

My penetrative understanding of the male mind would lead to my promotion to the rank of Commandress after the nuclear strikes. Before then, it led to me securing a husband.

I was married to a man with glasses and a moustache (unlike my subsequent house husband, It, this one was permitted to leave the house, to work for my benefit. Also, unlike It, he had his own name - although what that name was escapes me at this moment).

I was just a young girl, with low expectations of men, who was content to accept nightly foot rubs in place of compatibility or conversation. He was an older man with, it appears upon reflection, an all consuming foot fetish.

Each morning I'd find my shoes neatly arranged in rows. For dates he'd take me shoe shopping. He'd ask if he could cut my toenails for me. I'd tell him not while we were at the mall.

My husband came from the country we used to call Germany, before we realised that name was patriarchal and sexist and so changed it to Gerwomany. That name proved to be confusing, so now it's called Selma.

I did like that man's moustache. Maybe Dud, with his glasses and moustache reminded me of him. Who knows? Unlike the male mind, the female psyche is complex and impenetrable, and not easily digested in a two hour online Master's of Psychology.

He died in the first of the nuclear blasts...

Speaking of digestible, the self service hot-dog stand dispensed two sausages in bread and then fired out simultaneous streams of ketchup and mustard. In trying, and failing, to catch the sausages, with the baby still strapped to his torso, Dud allowed his arms to be covered in the red and yellow sauces, and then sprayed with fried onions and sliced gherkin.

Yes, I missed my husband very much.

*

"How's the hot-dog? Dud asked, as we seated ourselves on an elegantly carved park bench.

"It's not a cock-dog, but it will do," I answered, mouthing the mound of meat and sauce and fried onion suggestively.

"What are they doing?" asked Dud, blushing delightfully and trying to change the subject.

He pointed to a group of Studs, attired in their usual red tunics, yonder on the green, bending over in synchronisation.

"Pilates in the park," I explained.

"What are they being punished for?" Dud asked.

"They're not being punished. They're doing it voluntarily. The Studs these days, they're a disappointing bunch," I sighed as we observed further red-clad males taking pictures of their Commandresses - women of advanced age and official garb propped against and upon trees - trying to outdo each other for the most seductive shot.

I could tell Dud was confused by the whole scene. The site of Commandresses straddling branches and grinding against trees was a curious one.

"No female action is intended for the benefit of the man she is currently with," I explained. "Try to see it without the lens of your toxic entitlement."

Dud nodded, furrowing his brow in deep contemplation.

"A woman needs to feel wanted, desired. The fertilisation ceremony isn't enough. That's duty," I continued. "We've been trying to teach them how to wolf-whistle. It comes out like…"

I blew a long and deliberate raspberry to illustrate my point vividly, forgetting that my mouth was still full of hot-dog.

"They fail to satisfy us in every way. There is such a thing as foreplay. We like to play games, dressing up, role-play…"

"You mean like Dungeons and Dragons?"

"Does that involve pain and chains?" I asked.

"It can do."

And then, looking at him straight in the eye, tossing my hair over my shoulders and wiping my face, I asked:

"Do you want to play with me, Dud Wimpole?"

CHAPTER TEN

I'M FIFTY SHADES OF HOT

When I entered his shadowy bedroom, I found Mr. Wimpole standing by the window, arms crossed behind his back, gazing out into the blackness.

"Are you admiring your helicopter?" I asked.

"What helicopter?" he replied.

It was then that he truly noticed me, for he shuddered in excitement at the very sight of my curvaceous form. I rubbed my back against the frame of the doorway, showing off my contours, and scratching an itch that had teased me all day.

I wore transparent lingerie, no more than a thread, wrapped around my voluptuous body, and I had brought a sack of erotic toys.

I allowed the sack to drop to the floor, like a seductive Santa, and I bent over the dresser table.

"Spank me, Mr. Wimpole," I told him.

"Mr.? Is that term allowed?" he asked.

"Rules are meant to be broken, Mr. Wimpole - you taught me that - and so am I. Spank me."

"Are you sure?" he teased.

"I've never been as sure of anything in my life. Spank me!"

Dud patted my buttocks with his feeble palm, causing but a ripple.

Who was this twerp in spectacles, this tormentor of my soul?

"Spank me harder! Spank me again," I cried.

"I did," Dud advised.

"You're going to have to spank me harder than that. I didn't feel a thing. Try the sack," I ordered.

Dud rummaged through the sack of trusted arousal aids and pulled out an umbrella.

"Hit me with it!" I demanded.

Dud swung the umbrella across my buttocks, unleashing a war cry, and snapping the thing in two.

Still, I did not feel a thing.

The war cry, more of a scream, really, awoke the baby in the next room, which began to cry. Time was of the essence.

"Hurry, Dud," I told my sweating sex companion. "Excavate the dust from my loins!"

Dud collected a night stool from the dresser and charged at me with full speed.

He and the night stool bounced off my exterior, propelled across the room, and crashed into the dresser-mirror.

The baby was screaming now.

"Do it, Wimpole," I roared.

Dud dragged the wooden cello from the corner of the room and - using a might I never thought he possessed - swung the thing across my expectant rump.

It splintered upon impact, fracturing into a thousand

pieces, while the exhausted Wimpole collapsed to the floor.

"That's it. Go and see to that damn brat," I ordered, and I marched from the room, sensually unappeased, but at least with my dignity intact.

*

What was it about this scrawny little man with glasses that drove me so wild? This, I asked myself, as I lit a cigarette and regained my composure.

At first, I thought it was just the regular disappointment that a Stud had failed to impregnate me.

In a society that's 90% barren, there's status to be gained in producing a child.

But the irk that this man created in me ran deeper.

You must understand, dear reader, that my role in this society is to keep order and control.

I was affected by the personal blow this Dud had caused me in escaping the city, escaping my clutches, as well as what his actions meant to the order of this society as a whole.

Ever since he escaped Dileag, from the moment he fled my command, he had become an obsession.

I wanted to control him. I wanted to break him. I wanted to make him squirm.

I wanted to take his love for me and use it to make him suffer.

I am a woman who always gets what she wants.

*

On the way back to my boudoir, I stopped by the doorway of the nursery. I remained in the shadows, observing the curious Wimpole as he placed a hand on the sobbing child.

"There, there, Baby Dud," he said. "Let me read you a story. What do we have here?"

Dud took a children's book from the nursery table, sat down in a rocking chair beside the crib, and began to read:

"Snow White and the Seven Dwarfs,

With revisions by the Ministry of Culture.

Once upon a time, there was a wise and noble Queen, who spent all her days speaking to her mirror, which is a perfectly fine way to spend one's time.

The King hired a man to stand behind the mirror and tell the Queen how "fair" she was, making the Queen believe that the mirror was talking to her, so that the King would have the space and time to go out and fight the death defying battles that paid for the Queen's jewellery.

In other words, all was well in the Kingdom.

One day, the Queen found out that her wicked husband had fathered a child in a previous marriage, because that was the sort of thing men got up to in those times, and that the child was coming to live in the castle.

The child was called Snow White, and named after the whiteness of her skin, which was fitting because she was an emotional vampire.

Snow White was young and beautiful and full of life, and the Queen was totally fine with this. She just didn't like how annoying she was.

Snow White learnt that the Queen just didn't like how annoying she was, because the Queen told her so, and so Snow White ran away.

Snow White spent the rest of her days as a live-in slave for a bunch of bizarre old dwarfs, at least three of whom were clinically insane, and who, despite working in a diamond mine, couldn't be bothered to hire a paid cleaner.

The Queen lived happily ever after talking to her mirror,

until the man standing behind it died of malnutrition.

The moral of this story is clear.

The End."

Dud sat motionless for a few moments. Then he returned the book to the nursery table, and, leaning into the crib, placed a hand on the sleeping child's head.

"Don't worry, Baby Dud," I heard him whisper. "I'm going to get you out of this madhouse. I'm going to get you out of Dileag, even if it's the last thing I do."

And in that moment I was reminded of a fact as old as time itself: I, Commandress Roseanne, would have to destroy Dud Wimpole.

CHAPTER ELEVEN

I DESERVE MORE

As I lay on my bed dying, I look back on my journey and I ask, what kind of life was this? Did I do myself proud? Could I have done more? Been more? Probably not. I always... wait, no, what's this? Perhaps I am not dying. It turns out I just had gas.

So I get out of bed and start the day.

But what kind of day is this? What kind of day will it be?

And then I recall, Dud Wimpole has returned to my life.

It will be a shit day.

At least there is breakfast.

Dud awaited at the table, trying to prevent the "Baby Dud" beside him from committing suicide with the cutlery.

During his absence, I had dug deeper into the history of this Dud Wimpole. Who was this man who had affected me so: he who had resisted my powers, escaped my control, sacrificed my charms?

It turned out he was born shortly after the nuclear war. His infancy was spent in the tunnels.

When the people emerged into the daylight, and the children were sent to schools, Dud proved to be an average student. For his final essay in high school, he provided a breakdown of the plot to an old television episode - "Star Trek - The Day of the Triffids." There was no analysis. No commentary. Just a statement, beat by beat, on what happened in the episode. The boy was an idiot.

After that he was assigned an office job in the Ministry of Sending Endless Compliments, a card and phone message service created to boost the morale of the female leaders of the new world.

The only comment on his performance in the role was found in an annual appraisal form. It stated, "Is often late back from lunch." Failing in his role at the Ministry, he was appointed a role in the Office of Photoshopping Models to Appear Fatter, given a standard 2x2 metre apartment and left to lead an average life until the Great Roundup - called as such because men were rounded up (and assigned as Duds and Studs) and because it was great.

Regarding the Ministry of Sending Endless Compliments, because I am often questioned on this: that was one of the first Ministries set up under the new world order, and its establishment was not accomplished without comments from certain naysayers.

Some traditionalists suggested that requiring a government department to send inane flatteries to the women of society each day would undermine the clear independence and superiority of our gender.

It transpired, though, that following the establishment of the Ministry, admittance to hospitals was halved, A and E visits cut by two thirds and appointments at GPs reduced by 90%.

Having an endless stream of compliments being served incessantly negated the need for ladies to seek attention from the oversubscribed medical services, and so the Ministry of Sending Endless Compliments stands, inarguably, as one of our great, early success stories.

Personally, I've never suffered from attention deficit disorder. Men have always given me lots of attention. I have, they say, a vivacious personality. And they are drawn to my fulsome, big boned figure. They can't resist.

How had he escaped me, though? How had this unimpressive little man escaped Dileag? The question plagued me until it became all consuming and had me resolving to lure him back. Then I would inspect him, locked in my grasp, like a bug under a microscope. Then I would crush him.

And there he was, at the breakfast table, whistling to himself.

I made no mention of the previous night's failings, allowing them to hang in the air like the smell of burnt sausages. Speaking of which, I rang the bell above the table to signal that breakfast should be served.

"Enjoy your breakfast," I told Dud, coquettishly. "If such a thing is possible. Loathe to think what he'll serve."

Chef Niko the 2nd slithered from the kitchen with a tray of edibles in one hand, a napkin in the other. A former, failed Stud, I had kept him on in my service after his predecessor, Chef Niko the 1st, met his end in the Wimpole instigated bombing of Dileag. I'm beginning to wonder if I have a soft spot for failures. Yes, that is it. If I do have any failing, it is that I am too kind.

"This morning, Commandress, I have prepared for you: kale and pear delight, broccoli leaf, minced spinach, lightly peppered. Seeds. For drinks, blended salmon and tomato skins."

Having made his announcement, Chef Niko 2 stood erect with immense pride.

"Chef Niko the 2nd, this is Dud Wimpole," I announced. "Dud Wimpole, this is Chef Niko the 2nd, the worst chef I have ever met in my life."

Chef Niko 2 burst into tears and ran into the kitchen.

Note to self: be less kind.

"See what I mean about Studs these days?" I pointed out. "Useless."

"What happened to the Uncles - those who used to train the Studs?" Dud asked.

"Bled dry," I told him, while trying to gnaw some kale.

"Bled dry?"

"Hung upside down. Their throats slit. The blood completely emptied from their body. Bled dry. Your escaping was in part blamed on a failure of their training, and any toxic who fails a Commandress is bled dry. Keep that in mind. Quick photo. Pretend to be loving it."

I took a quick snap of the three of us, myself, Dud and the baby, over the food. The looks on our faces betrayed that this concoction was anything but edible.

"Come," I said to Dud. "You're to go shopping for groceries with my latest Stud - Stud Buffcheeks. You'll need to wear the red garb of Studs in order to blend in. I'll introduce you."

*

"Shouldn't he be out of pampers, now?" Dud asked mysteriously, still struggling to place the red cloak of Studs over his head, as I led him to the outdoor gymnasium.

"Who?" I asked.

"The baby."

"If he was out of pampers he'd shit everywhere!"

I get irritable when I haven't eaten.

We found Stud Buffcheeks in his usual spot, under the bench press in the outdoor gymnasium - the converted yard.

Stud Buffcheeks was a short, squat man, with a gym-built body and tattoos on his biceps. He sprang up when he saw me approaching, stood to attention, and saluted.

"Stud Buffcheeks at attention and reporting to duty, mam."

A bit embarrassing, really.

"At ease, Buffcheeks," I told him. "This is Dud Wimpole. Dud will be staying with us, temporarily, maybe longer, as long as he pleases me."

"The Commandress is wise in her ways and shall be trusted in all of her decisions," Buffcheeks responded, going red with jealousy, and clasping Dud's hand warmly until a crack was heard.

"You toxics head out and get me some food. Take the baby with you. Leave him here and I'll probably eat him. Be late home and I'll have you both bled dry."

Then, turning to Dud, I added:

"Stud Buffcheeks is everything a Commandress would want from a Stud. He keeps in shape. He had penis implants so he could reach my nether-regions. He lets me sit on his face while I take conference calls. But he isn't you."

I still don't know what I meant by, "he isn't you," and I don't know why I said it, but the awkwardness, and downright strangeness of this statement hung in the air for a while, over all of us, and was only broken when Dud resumed whistling.

I took a quick group selfie and sent them on their way.

*

Reflecting upon my behaviour in the days following Dud Wimpole's return, it is clear to me that I was under a great deal of stress. The pressure of managing a society, a home and a rich and romantic love life can take its toll. One must keep it together. One must keep it together. One must keep it together.

You see, dear reader, it wasn't always this way. Things were different before we took the management of the world under our care. Back then, and throughout much of human history, the ultimate aim of most females was to live the life of an overgrown leech. She would achieve this by granting males occasional access to her waste-disposal orifices.

I believe the pop group, The Sneaky Leeches, said it best with their song, "State of the Union:"

"U want dis sloppy ass pussy

U want dis pussy

U want dis pussy

U gotta put dem dollars in da pussy boy."

The fact that this was an anthem for my generation during its adolescence accurately reveals the prevailing culture of those days.

But now we were different. We were independent. We were proud. We were running the world. We were composed. We were calm. We were in control. We were accomplished. We were stable. We were on top. Our lower organs were used solely for the reproductive powers which would save our species, and still for defecation and urination, but not for charming men.

Incidentally, each of the Sneaky Leeches aspired to be a Commandress in the new world order. Each was refused the honor on account of their collective ovaries having experienced so many cumulative abortions that no Leech would be likely to bear a child, depriving the former pop princesses the potential to fulfill the complete and highest duties of the Commandress role.

l think this goes to show, ladies, the truth in the old

adage: that you can flaunt the powers of your pussy all you want in youth, deliberately making that slightly chubbier girl in gym class feel bad, but one day that chubby but pretty girl will rise to a position that you can only aspire to, and she will look down upon you from a great height, from her golden throne, bitches!

Oh yes, for many women, having a man sniffing around their private parts, driving them to the stores, carrying their shopping and driving them home, was enough in the way of flattery and status to constitute a life. Some of us, however, aspired to more. Some of us would rise above. Some of us would taste greatness.

I was on the shitter when I got the call from the local fire department. Dud Wimpole had been caught up one of their ladders, propped against the city wall, trying to escape Dileag.

CHAPTER TWELVE

I AM A STRONG AND CAPABLE WOMAN

"Do you think your toxic is capable of deception?"

That was the question asked of me by Fire Captain Commandress Chambers, Director of the Fire Department, Head of Public Diversity and Executive Director of Dileag Bake Sales, as we stood at the foot of the ladder Dud had propped up against the city wall.

A group of us stood there: myself and Commandress Chambers, Dud and Stud Buffcheeks, Chantelle playing with her phone, the venerable and withered retired General Commandress Nancy who had been rescued from a fire above the grocery shop, smoke still billowing from her clothes, all awaiting my answer (apart from Chantelle).

"Do you think your toxic is capable of deception?" Fire Captain Commandress Chambers asked again, stroking her round belly, looking like she was ready to give birth at any second.

All members of the fire department were heavily pregnant, of course.

It had been observed that in the time of toxic rule, all

women in the later stages of pregnancy had been excluded from emergency response roles in fire departments - another form of repression.

As a correction, now all emergency response roles in the fire department were staffed by women in the later stages of pregnancy, which, in these barren times, pretty much amounted to all the women in later stages of pregnancy in Dileag.

The initiative didn't do much to alleviate infant mortality rates in the city, but it sure as hell made a point!

The way Dud told it, a fire broke out in the apartment above the grocery shop when Dud and Buffcheeks happened to be walking by, shopping for eggs, a fire caused by one of the ancient General's cigars. The fire department arrived, and with the pregnant fire crew unable to make it up more than two rungs of the ladder, they had instead turned their attention to callisthenics in a huddle on the floor.

This much was corroborated by the still huddled women, doing their breathing exercises, in full fire uniform, on the floor by the building. The fire still raged overhead.

This is where the story gets hazy. According to the deeply senile General Commandress Nancy, Dud Wimpole broke into her apartment and pulled her from the fire in an attempt to "ravish her."

With the aid of Buffcheeks, Dud had made it down the ladder with the ancient General, and depsite the protestations of Buffcheeks, Dud had then propped and climbed the ladder against the city wall, the Baby Dud still strapped to his chest, to, as he claims, "get a better view."

Did I believe Dud Wimpole was capable of deception?

"No, I don't think he is," I answered.

"What?" Fire Captain Chambers guffawed. "Can it be - a Commandress who is being controlled by her toxic? Look at him, there, with his glasses!"

It seems hard to believe I had allowed things to go this far, I know. But the alternative was harder for me to accept in that moment: that Dud Wimpole was again trying to escape me.

"I am in control, here," I bellowed, shoving my bosom into the face of Captain Chambers. "I will not be betrayed, I demand loyalty and I will prove it!"

*

I responded with action that was both swift and severe, yet perfectly justifiable.

The look on that bespectacled bastard's face, as he stared up at me with his usual blank and beady-eyed expression triggered something in me.

In my mind, I suddenly associated Dud Wimpole's subordination with the fact that he wore glasses.

So, here's what I did.

I rounded up all the toxics at the Gonad Assessment Centre who wore glasses, prior to them even being tested for fertility, and I ordered Dud Wimpole to execute them all.

This would be the ultimate test of loyalty.

Myself, Fire Captain Chambers, a shaven-headed armed guard, and Dud with Baby Dud stood at one end of the converted cow shed that is the Gonad Assessment Centre.

We congregated behind the transparent control panel - resembling a DJ deck - with mighty cogs visible inside.

The testees entered: a group of hopeless, bespectacled, certain-to-be-Duds, soon-to-be-slaughtered toxics. They took their place in individual cubicles along the two inner sides of the barn.

The guard flicked a switch on the control panel and the

iron door at the opposite end of the barn slammed shut.

I looked at Fire Captain Chambers with a knowing wink and then addressed my audience.

"Testees. I know that you have been rounded up, taken from your regular lives, and that normally, you would be here to be tested for fertility, and so assigned as Studs or Duds," I began. "However, to pay for the indiscretions of Dud Wimpole, your fellow glasses wearer, to my left, you will now all be executed."

The testees let out an exhausted groan. They were clearly disappointed.

"I will now pull the switch to put the gun-bags in place. You may pretend to be eating swill, if it takes your minds off... having your minds being taken off," I quipped.

I find a little joke can ease even the most messy of situations.

I pulled a switch, causing deep house music to blast through the place. I quickly turned it off.

"Sorry, sorry. This place doubles as a nightclub, at night. It's a really happening place, you would have loved it," I explained.

See, I can be fun, too?

I pulled a different switch and individual guns, hidden behind swill bags, lowered down to each cubicle, pointing at the testees, at head height.

"Dud Wimpole will now pull the trigger."

The guard pulled a lever and the cogs within the control panel began to turn. She indicated to Dud a switch on the panel to fire the weapons.

Fire Captain Chambers cast an admiring glance my way and it felt good.

She, the guard and I retreated to a screened booth to avoid blood splattering on our clothes. I took a quick selfie to capture the moment: the three of us, and in the background - Dud at the control panel, the soon to be shot testees beyond him - excellent.

Dud turned white.

He cast a glance my way. I cocked my fingers as though they were a gun and aimed them at Baby Dud's head. My point was made.

The brat responded with two sucks of his pacifier, which he then seemingly spat in my direction.

Dud turned his attention to the testees and mouthed the words, "I'm sorry."

He leaned over the control panel and placed his hands on the switch.

Then, in a moment of bad luck or innate ineptitude, Dud Wimpole's glasses fell into the control panel causing an eruption of sparks and malfunction.

The house music blasted on and disco lights flashed across the insides of the barn. The great iron door began opening and closing and opening…

The testees looked to Dud in goggle eyed confusion.

Dud pointed to the door.

The testees cheered and began their stampede to the exit.

Dud Wimpole looked my way and merely shrugged.

*

The television cameras captured everything.

With the Dileag sky-line as a backdrop, bespectacled testees poured out of the Gonad Assessment Centre and into the evening-light.

Music pumped from the building.

Nightclub spot-lights beamed from the roof, across the sky.

The testees, arms at their sides, running with the gait of

headless chickens, unfamiliar with their freedom, scattered in all directions.

I was in trouble.

CHAPTER THIRTEEN

I AM PERFECTLY STABLE

A curious dream visited me in the darkness, a dream in which I am dressed in the red drag of a male - a Stud.

I appear to be in the Stud training centre, post gonadal assessment.

The bell that measures time is ringing. Time here is measured by bells, as once in nunneries. As in a nunnery too, there are few mirrors.

I get up out of a chair, advance my feet into the sunlight, in their red shoes, flat-heeled to save the spine and not for dancing. The red gloves are lying on a bed. I pick them up, pull them onto my hands, finger by finger. Everything except the wings around my face is red: the colour of blood, which defines us. The skirt is ankle-length, full, gathered to a flat yoke that extends over the breasts, the sleeves are full. The white wings too are prescribed issue; they are to keep us from seeing, but also from being seen. I never looked good in red, it's not my colour.

The clock that tells the time is ticking. The bell that makes a ding is dinging. The nuns who live in the nunnery are nunning. I long for a mirror.

I get up out of the chair using my body. I put one foot in front of the other and then another. I repeat this action. In short, I am walking. I am walking in red shoes. These shoes are not made for dancing. The shoes are red, the gloves are red, the gown is red. My nose is red. I have a cold. The gown is flat yoke, covering and rising to the teet. I don't know what this means. The cold has gone to my head. I don't like red. That rhymes. Now, I am a poet and I don't know it.

What could it possibly mean?

Oh, how I love to write!

I do hope that I will have you there forever, my dear, reading whatever I write down, nodding in appreciation and agreement.

I spent the morning contemplating how best to enact revenge on Dud Wimpole for releasing a flock of bespectacled testees into the city the day before. While doing so, I inflicted perhaps the grandest revenge of all: I gave him the silent treatment.

Dud pottered about the mansion tending to the baby while I observed the round-up of the testees on the tele-screen. The round-up was swift and easy. Most of the testees handed themselves in wilfully. They had nowhere else to go. They had no hope. We had conditioned them well.

I decided to avoid going to the Command Centre until the whole thing boiled over.

Nothing pleases the fellow Commandresses more than when one of their number has had a mishap. I would ride this one out, and return to gloat when one of the fellow leaders had befallen their own disaster. That, at least, was the plan.

In the meantime, I employed some trusted coping techniques.

Whenever one encounters a burden or a situation that may not go to one's liking, I find that sometimes it's best to just scream.

When feeling slightly overwhelmed or perturbed, I like to retire to the ladies room and scream at the top of my lungs, and whatever I'm having to deal with, that helps.

Try it, dear reader. It works.

I often supplement the screams by shaking my cheeks to and fro and making the sound - "wibble wobble, wibble wobble," - and concluding by pulling out tufts of my hair and in severe cases, slamming my head into the toilet bowl.

I'd spent the night enjoying one such program of self-wellness therapy and so was able to face the following day composed, calm and back to my true self.

I covered up the bruises on my forehead by combing my hair over into a fringe and applying an extra layer of blemish across my eyebrows, which, if I may say so, made me look even more beautiful than I had before, and it was no surprise that Dud couldn't keep his eyes off the upper region of my head when he encountered me in the living room.

The morning calm was broken by the sound of a limousine pulling up outside the mansion. The door car slammed and was followed by the unmistakable sound of cracking walnuts.

It was Mother.

*

Mother entered, throwing her cloak at Chantelle with one hand and, as always, cracking walnuts with her diamond studded metal tongs in the other.

I asked Mother once if she used to crack walnuts constantly in order to intimidate men. She responded by pointing out that she didn't need to crack walnuts to be able to intimidate men.

She had a point. Even my stuffed former husband on the wall looked intimidated - and he was dead!

She stood, dressed in black, head to toe, tunic, headscarf and heels, 6 foot 7, with the cold, hard stare of a woman who hasn't been laid in a very long time.

"How are you, daughter?" she asked.

"Menstruating," I told her. "How are you?"

"Menopause," she told me.

A gulp sounded from the corner of the room, reminding me that there was Dud, entertaining the baby, on the floor. I indicated that he should stand.

"This is my mother, Chief Commandress Germaine. Ah, Mother, this is my, my…"

"Yes, I've heard all about your relationship with this thing," Mother announced. "I take it this is the one who caused the trouble last time. In fact, I have just come from the Command Centre. Your colleagues tell me you haven't been seen for days."

"Well, I've been very busy."

"They also told me that a mysterious new house guest has entered your life, and that yesterday, you were responsible for unleashing a gaggle of Duds into the city."

"Very busy and overloaded."

"You are at risk of losing your position, my daughter, a position that was bestowed on you by my generosity, and I can not let that happen."

"I don't know what to do, Mother," I admitted.

"I believe it was the great dramatist, Olivia Wilde, who once wrote, if I can't be famous, I'll be infamous. I'll tell you what you'll do, you'll secure a promotion."

"A promotion, Mother?"

"Yes, you'll be promoted from being a lowly Commandress to being an all powerful… Influencer!"

With that, Mother - Chief Commandress Germaine - let out a triumphant, maniacal laugh to the heavens, the kind she used to reserve for the four or five times a day I would soil my pamper as a child, meaning that father would have to change me - back when we were a normal family.

*

Mother, myself, Dud and the baby took our places round the dining table for a hastily assembled planning meeting, and brunch. This was all rather exciting.

"We will invite a film crew into your home to film you 24 hours a day. The Commandress and her toxic, a curious relationship. We will film endless videos of you gyrating your hips and serve them to kindergarten children via apps. You will be present on all media, at all times. And when we have the eyes of the world on you, your toxic, and his insubordination, will be made an example of. He will be broken for the entire world to see."

"Pleased to meet you," Dud said finally.

I could see that they would get along.

"Well, daughter, you certainly have an unusual relationship with your household. I understand that your feelings were hurt by his running away, but I fail to see how this solves matters."

"But Mother, will people watch?" I asked, trying to change the subject.

"Not only will they watch: they won't stop watching! There will be a morbid fascination amongst the people for your involvement with this thing. They'll follow your every action, hooked on the will she, won't she - slaughter him -

dynamic. And if ratings and responses fall below 90% of the population we will answer that yes she will!"

"Brunch is served," announced Chef Niko the 2nd.

The lanky chef glided out of the kitchen with the usual proud look upon his face. He placed a tray of curiosities on our table which I immediately feared would not please our guest.

"Chief Commandress Germaine. Commandress Roseanne. I present to you an array of leaves: boiled fig leaf, oak leaf and carrot leaf, sprinkled with birch pine, complemented by ground herbs in cactus water," he said, sealing his own fate.

Mother stood up and smashed the plate over the head of Chef Niko the 2nd.

"If my chef served me food like this I would have him bled dry!"

"I'm sorry, Mother," I told her.

"Well, what are we waiting for?" she asked. "Have him taken outside right this minute. We'll have ourselves a bleeding!"

CHAPTER FOURTEEN

I AM ON THE CUSP OF GREATNESS

Things were getting worse for me.

Mother had Stud Buffcheeks drag Chef Niko the 2nd out to the yard and tie him upside down from some monkey bars.

"I can make vegetable souffle, powder grains, dried tempe…" Chef Niko the 2nd was saying.

"String him higher," Mother ordered.

Stud Buffcheeks pulled on the rope around Niko the 2nd's legs so that the chef's neck was at a nice comfortable height for Mother.

Chantelle ran over from washing the limo to witness the spectacle.

"I can make soy sandwiches, pumpkin soup, dandelion petals…" Chef Niko 2 continued.

It was pathetic.

Mother clicked her fingers and an eighteen inch blade dropped from her sleeve into her hand.

"Oh, please, please don't do this." Niko the 2nd was embarrassing me, now.

Mother took position, ready to strike.

"Stop! Wait!" I screamed. "Please, all of you, wait!"

I handed Buffcheeks my phone.

"Quick photo," I ordered.

Mother and I stood by the upside down Niko 2. Chantelle joined us.

"Say drained," I laughed.

"Drained," the four of us said.

And then Mother sliced open Niko the 2nd's throat with her blade.

Blood spilled to the floor.

"One more group photo," I suggested.

"Not now," said Mother, standing back to admire her work.

She had sliced well.

"Your father was completely drained, you know?" she said, using her archaic euphemism for "bled dry," and never missing an opportunity to remind me of this nugget of family history.

I could recite the details by heart. Mother had asked Father if he thought a young beauty queen on the television was prettier than her. He foolishly answered, in a moment of madness, with:

"Yes, of course she is."

Mother drained him herself.

And this was back in the days of the Oppressive Patriarchy when a female slaughtering a male was severely frowned upon in a court of law.

Our reminiscing was interrupted by the barking of the guard dogs.

"What's wrong with them?" asked Mother.

"That'll be Dud trying to escape again." I told her.

"Well round him up. We have work to do."

*

We went to the University to recruit our media crew. We would need a team to broadcast our every moment, around the clock, and we would tap into their generational adeptness on how to use technology to influence and empower.

When we arrived on campus, young female students were walking to and fro in bright gowns and outrageous hats, all trying to outdo one another. There was not a toxic in sight. It really was an inspirational environment.

Mother and I let ourselves into the lecture theatre. I pulled Dud along on a lead. He still had that damn baby with him.

A lecture had begun, delivered by the venerable Professor Commandress Margaret.

"Tell me," she began. " How many of you are in this class because your mother bribed me?"

All five hundred hands in the audience were raised.

"Congratulations, you've all got A's," Professor Commandress Margaret announced.

A cheer erupted from the auditorium and the students got to their feet.

"Wait!" ordered Mother, as she led myself and Dud onto the stage. "Sit down."

Dud sat down, cross-legged on the stage.

"Not you, Dud," I told him.

"Chief Commandress Germaine," Professor Commandress Margaret announced. "What an honour!"

"Apologies for bringing a toxic control freak onto campus," Mother began. "He couldn't be trusted to be alone. Watch him! If he starts to masturbate compulsively, let me know. I'll have him completely drained."

Dud waived to the audience.

"How many of you know how to use a camera?" Mother asked.

Five hundred hands went up.

"How many of you know how to point a camera at something other than yourselves?"

All but five hands went down.

"Good. You five have been selected for a mission of national importance. The rest of you join me in prayer."

The students bowed their heads.

"I am a victim, I am a victim, I am a victim," Mother began, with the students repeating in loyal reverence. "It is the right of every woman to have something pass in or out of at least one of her orifices, at all times. Praise the vulva."

"Praise the vulva," the audience chimed back.

Mother then turned to me.

"Show time."

It is interesting to reflect, dear reader, on what became a turning point in my life.

Some Commandresses crave the attention that the position brings. Not me.

I simply fed on the enjoyment and power of telling people what to do and the pleasure and eroticism of telling people what not to do.

That moment, though, when mother told me that I was to become a reality media star and "Influencer," began a desire for blind celebrity fame that has cursed me ever since.

*

Mother picked the brains of our new, highly qualified media team and presented her broadcast plan in my living room.

Meanwhile, Dud and Baby Dud crouched on the floor, deeply engaged in the futile and inane exercise of building things out of minuscule bricks.

Idiots.

"The centre piece will be the 24 hour reality broadcast of your life, detailing the life of a Commandress with her Stud. We've ordered the media channels to start broadcasting tomorrow."

"Divine," I told Mother.

"We'll supplement this with a constant stream of lurid content distributed through phone apps such as Cok-Cok."

"Cok-Cok, Mother?" I asked.

"Commandresses upload videos of themselves gyrating their hips. Viewers show their approval by sending back photos of their cocks. Whoever gets sent the most cocks wins."

"Jealous?" I asked Dud.

"I pity the both of you," he said.

"I knew he'd be jealous," I told Mother.

"Most viewers are Duds currently sweeping nuclear waste, counting down the hours to death, sending cock photos in their down time. They're exactly the audience we want to warn against uprising, and we will do that by showing the destruction of your subservient, here."

"I think we've lost a wheel," Dud blurted out, inexplicably.

"But what about the rest of the population?" I asked.

"They'll be tuning in for the reality show. The news agencies are to read a press release this evening announcing that your newly returned Stud was indeed he who fled Dileag those years ago, and that the repercussions will be played out for all to see."

"I'm ready!" I told Mother.

"Not quite," she advised. "First we need to get you into

hair and make-up, and then we need to suck 90% of the fat from your buttocks and inject it into your lips.Then we need to suck 100% of the fat from your thighs, and inject it into your buttocks."

And so began my new life.

CHAPTER FIFTEEN

I AM A STAR

We shot the opening credit sequence for the reality show overnight. The theme was: the cast assembles for a family photo.

Mother stood at the back, all stern and severe.

Stud Buffcheeks was to play the dour and deadpan one. He delivered the line:

"Somebody make me laugh."

Chantelle held the baby up to the camera for its close-ups.

Dud tried to run off during filming. We used that in the sequence.

I was the curvaceous, kooky, coquettish one - what we call in the industry a "three dimensional character" - and while showing off my curves to the camera, I said, laughingly:

"That Dud, always trying to escape!"

Then we held up the title card: "Keeping Up With The Commandresses."

I watched the sequence air live on a monitor backstage -

I mean in my yard - before making my entrance for the opening scene.

The living room had been transformed into a film studio. The five recruits from the University were crammed into the corners of the room, holding cameras, lighting and microphones, hiding from view behind sofas.

My brief was to "try to act natural, and pretend I have just been out shopping at some of our sponsors." It wasn't easy to act natural in that setting!

When I entered, Dud had been positioned over the coffee table and, under orders, was trying, and failing, to perform bicep curls. Act natural indeed!

He let out a startled squeak when I entered and I realised that it was at the sight of my face.

The liposuction-lip-inflation had been a great success, but clearly it was hard for Dud to take in my transformation all at once.

"So, I just got back from the Prada store. I got their new line," I said, holding up a Prada bag to the camera.

Dud just froze. He gave nothing back.

"So, how was your day?" I prompted.

Nothing - I got zero from him - a deer in the headlights.

"Great," I covered. "Then I went to Gucci and got this awesome jacket. What do you think?"

I held up a bright green jacket with a tiger print on the back.

Still no response from Dud.

"Awesome!" I said. "Well, I'm going to take a shower and then you can take me to Lava. It's like, the hottest place in the city."

A star was born, dear reader.

*

Lava restaurant at night: dark, jazzy and cool. I immediately felt that I belonged.

"Dinner for two, film crew of five," I told the Stud concierge as we entered.

I was doused in my favourite perfumes, while Dud had dressed up for the affair in his preferred blue swimming shorts and black t-shirt under a red gown. We made quite the spectacle. Ratings would be through the roof!

Lava is popular, of course, because instead of tables and chairs (boring!) diners lay flat on elevated beds and are served into their mouths by Stud waiters wearing nothing but aprons. I had been dying to try the place.

Dud and I lay down on our respective beds and basked in the scene.

"Ludicrous," observed Dud.

"Say something fascinating," I told him. "To the camera. Entertain me."

"Surely only a pervert would be watching this," he offered.

Thankfully, we were saved by our Stud waiter, presenting a bottle with a flourish.

"Would the toxic care to test the wine to check that it has not been poisoned?" he asked.

"Yes, he would," I commanded.

The Stud poured a sample of wine into a glittering glass and handed it to Dud. Leaning over on one elbow, Dud had a sip, and promptly choked up the fluid like a malfunctioning fountain.

"How is it?" asked the Stud.

"Ridiculous," Dud answered.

"I will return with your menus, Commandress," the Stud announced, leaving with a bow.

It was at this moment, that Dud Wimpole finally took action, putting into place what I realised was his plan all along.

A tinkling sound on the floor indicated that something had dropped from his pocket, something eye-catching: some fake looking pearls, a roll of glasses repair tape, and most significantly, an engagement ring, designed in the erotic style of a nipple hook.

"What was that - that ring?" I asked, as Dud hopped off the table and scrambled on the floor.

"Oh, nothing," he gushed, before adding incoherently, "I must have picked it up with a Beyonce burger."

Then, looking at him down there on one knee, I realised why the kinky bastard was babbling so, and what he was truely up to.

"Oh, my word," I exclaimed, and perhaps with less consideration that I should have given the decision, I announced, "I do!"

Lava erupted into a roar of approval.

The Stud waiters joined in an impromptu rendition of a Korean pop dance.

And just like that, dear reader, I was engaged to be married.

*

My immediate thought upon my engagement was, "I'll never have to work again." I admit, this had no bearing on reality. It was a throwback to the past - cultural conditioning - and for this I am ashamed.

I would have to continue my essential work as a Commandress whether I was married or not, and Dud would remain in the mansion, albeit as a house husband, doing nothing all day.

Maybe those pre-nuclear war women were on to something, though. Theirs was a society in which the majority of male labour was directed at financing the comfort of a female.

And maybe by accessing the finances and labour of a male, in terms of leisure time, these women effectively doubled their life-span.

I quickly dispelled thoughts like this as pernicious conditioning whenever they'd enter my mind.

We, the women of the present, had got things right. We would spend our days at work, commuting and in meetings. They, the women of the past, had wasted their lives on rest, relaxation and self-indulgence. They had got things wrong.

Dud went straight to his room immediately upon arrival home, seemingly drunk and confused from the sip of wine.

Mother was waiting for me in the living room. She was cracking walnuts fervently.

She sent the film crew outside to film Chantelle trying, and failing, to park the car.

"Mother, you saw the good news. We must begin to plan…" I remember saying.

"The ratings are atrocious!" Mother announced. "Nobody is subscribing to your feeds. Your girations have received but five cocks - and they were all limp! You do not have an audience!"

"What if I show more anus?"

"You have shown all of your anus," she pointed out. "One of the Duds complimented you on your anus in a Cok-Cok message. We had him completely drained for objectifying you. Don't you remember?"

"I can't remember everything, Mother. Excuse me, but I have a finite brain."

"That was this afternoon."

"Curse those Duds!" I cried.

"It seems that the novelty of a fat lady and her twerp has run out," Mother lamented. "We must do more."

I gulped.

"You don't mean you want us to release a sex tape?" I asked.

"Every mother in the city has released a sex tape of her daughter at one time or another," Mother began. "No, we must go straight to the endgame."

"The endgame?" I asked.

"The endgame," she began. "Dud Wimpole is going to have to have gender reassignment surgery."

CHAPTER SIXTEEN

I AM A WOMAN ON TOP

Today, I discovered that if I arch my back as far as possible and stand at an angle to a camera or mirror, my body looks like an inverted S, and is quite delectable.

If you hold the following up to a mirror, you'll see what I mean.

S

You're welcome.

It's never easy telling a man that he is to be filmed having gender reassignment surgery in order to increase televisual viewer ratings.

If I have any advice, if you find yourself in the same position as I, it would be to just go for it. Rip the plaster off. He will understand.

Probably.

Dud was in bed reading "Davina Copperfield" by nightlight when I entered his room.

"Dud, I'm cold. Can I come into your bed for a little

while? It's ok, you can continue reading."

Soften them up.

I climbed into bed with him.

"Ah, this is nice," I said, snuggling up to my frail fiance.

Dud didn't look up from the book.

"So, Mother wants you to have gender reassignment surgery," I began. "For the show. She wants your penis and testicles removed first, live. Then hormone treatment. Breast implants..."

Dud put the book down and sighed.

"I don't want this to happen either. I don't want to be married to a man with no testicles. Those balls are mine. I have a plan to make you more popular. It involves you reinventing yourself as a hip-hop artist, changing your name to D. Wimp, starting a clothing line, and a religion...."

Dud sprung up from his bed and left the room. He was clearly unhappy with all of this.

I found him in the baby's room, trying to awaken the child by lifting its hand.

"What are you doing?" I asked.

"I'm escaping, with Baby Dud."

"Baby Dud, Baby Dud! It's not your baby!" I screamed. "You're infertile! How could it be your baby? You're a Dud!"

"He looks just like me."

"Novelty glasses! You're delusional! This self-deception is why most toxics in the history of the world raised children that weren't even theirs. Male-ego! The baby is Stud Ramrod's."

Sometimes, you really have to spell it out to them.

"Ramrod's?" Dud asked.

"I wrote that letter so you'd come back to me! You think he chose this outfit himself? Beach shorts! I've got eyes everywhere. Women talk!"

I mean, really!

"Ok," said Dud.

"Why won't you love me? Tell me one thing wrong with me! Tell me one thing!" I pleaded.

"You're a psychopath."

"So?" I screamed.

Dud let the little hand of Baby Dud drop back to the bed. He kissed the child on the forehead, and then he silently left the room.

Dud Wimpole was a broken man.

I had destroyed him.

I had won.

*

The castration was arranged for the next morning.

An operating table was set up in the living room, medical instruments by the side, spotlight above.

Commandress Nurse Vera had been invited to perform the surgery. She arranged her instruments on a tray, filmed by the crew, and watched by Mother, cracking walnuts, and I in the corner of the room.

The baby played in his crib on the other side of the room. It was important that he see this - that all of Dileag see this.

Dud Wimpole entered in his nightgown. He looked… how should I describe this? Sad.

"Hello, there," said Commandress Nurse Vera, in her delightfully upbeat and caring tone. "You must be Dud Wimpole. I'm Commandress Nurse Vera. Do make yourself comfortable."

Dud climbed onto the operating table.

"Is this your first sex change?" Commandress Nurse Vera asked.

"Yes," Dud answered.

"Fine, fine. Nervous?"

"Yes," Dud answered again.

"No wonder. You are about to have your testicles cut off," joked the jolly nurse, getting a good laugh from the room.

She then positioned Dud's feet in metallic rests, to keep his legs up, and open.

"Don't worry, I'm highly experienced in these matters," said the nurse. "When I'm not chopping balls, I'm committing self-harm with knives, so you are in safe hands. Although, the same cannot be said for your testicles."

Another laugh rippled from those of us watching. This woman really was hilarious.

Commandress Nurse Vera turned to Mother and asked:

"Was it the whole genitalia? Not just testicles?"

Mother nodded in the affirmative.

"Whole cock and balls. That's lovely," the nurse said, and then turning to Dud: "I'm going to give you a localised injection rather than general anaesthetic. I'm told that you sleeping through the procedure won't make for great entertainment."

More laughter.

"Normally, I'd invite your partner to film the procedure, since this moment is something very special you share together, but I think the filming is taken care of for us."

She was on a roll!

"But she can sit by your side to give you comfort."

"No," Dud began, weakly.

I pulled over a chair and patted my little fiance on the head. I told him I was proud of him. Then I took a bite of the hot-dog I'd brought along to enjoy while watching the spectacle.

With a final sharpening of the scissors, Commandress

Nurse Vera declared:

"And so we will begin."

Commandress Nurse Vera leaned in with a syringe in one hand, a knife in the other.

And at that moment, whatever adhesive was holding my former husband, It, to the wall, gave way, and It crashed to the ground.

You can imagine my surprise - all of our surprise - when It got right up to his feet and dusted himself off.

*

Stud Buffcheecks rushed in, alerted by the commotion, followed by Chantelle.

"What is this?" demanded Mother. "Your husband is alive!"

"It?" I began. I didn't know what to say.

"And he's been watching us this whole time!" roared Mother.

"Hello, dear," said It, to me, in his familiar, sheepish tones.

"Well, not only do we get a live castration, we get ourselves a complete draining," Mother announced.

I admired Mother immensely. She really was an evil and formidable woman. No wonder she became a reality TV producer.

Taking his cue, Buffcheeks pulled a leather strap from the surgical table, wrapped it around It's legs, and hung my former husband upside down from the chandelier.

The camera crew got up close to capture the action.

Mother took centre position in the living room. Her blade dropped from her sleeve, gleaming.

"Stop! Wait! Wait!" I screamed. "Please, stop! Quick group photo."

I held out the phone for Dud to take.

And what happened next can only be described as an out of body experience.

I saw the whole scene as though from above.

There was It, swinging from the chandelier, Buffcheeks holding the leather strap. There was the film crew, capturing every second. There was Mother, poised to strike. There was Commandress Nurse Vera, looking on in shock. There was Chantelle gazing out of the window.

There was the crib, empty.

There was the operating table, vacated…

And above it all, I heard myself scream.

"Where the fuck is Dud Wimpole?"

PART THREE

GRENADES

A Testament by Stud Ramrod

CHAPTER SEVENTEEN

ALL ROADS

Our paths are intertwined, Dud Wimpole and I, like the limbs of two gladiators locked in an embrace.

Or like the roots of a tree, also locked in an embrace.

A male tree.

We're two sides of the same coin.

A golden medallion.

One of us is Dud Wimpole and the other is Stud Ramrod.

Although which is which has sometimes been up for debate.

What's for certain, though, is that he is our leader.

And our leader was on his way back to us.

And that only one of us had recently come out as a flaming homosexual.

I'm proud to say that one was me.

It was time to prepare the welcome party.

*

We knew Dud would find us.

"All roads lead to the same destination," my fellow hideouts told me.

"Great minds think alike," I joked, daring to align our minds with that of the hero himself, the special one, Dud Wimpole.

Realistically, there was only one place a man would hide in Dileag, where no woman would have any interest in going - the philosophy section at the back of the book shop.

It is where we had found safety.

The bombing had been a great success. We had flown those planes over the city, the menfolk of the household of Commandress Roseanne, It, Marku the maid, Chef Niko and I, with those who joined us, Stud Longun and Stud Mastall, the grocery shopping partners of Dud Wimpole.

We were a brave and brilliant battalion.

Dud Wimpole had single handedly distracted the eyes of the city to buy us the time to fire up the planes, fly them over the city, and unleash all the TNT we could carry onto the malls, boutiques and salons.

Some of us even managed to survive the landing.

Martial law was declared immediately. We found that by commandeering a tank, we could move around the city and fit right in.

Like Dud, we had tried the museum.

Boarded up.

We tried the art galleries.

Burned down.

The sports stadium.

That had been the sight of Dud's final battle.

It was being refitted for the following Sunday's bake sale.

And so to a forgotten book shop on the ground floor of the mall, abandoned and ignored, in plain view, but a neglected blind-spot between a perfume shop and a beauty salon.

The troops ordered to burn every book in Dileag written under the old order had torched the place up to the mid aisles, and had not cared to check if their work was done, distracted, most likely, by the shopping next door.

And Dud had followed our own footsteps into the shadows in search of a place to hide.

We watched on CCTV as Dud made his way through the city.

We watched as he ripped open his nightgown to reveal his t-shirt, with a ghost logo, underneath.

We watched him as he navigated his way into the mall, and to the back of the book shop, to the philosophy section, stealthily, like a bespectacled ninja.

Shoppers went to and fro, ignoring the place completely.

We watched him fireman carry that child over his shoulder, searching for safety, like a rescue hero in swim shorts.

Advertising screens across the city switched to the image of Dud Wimpole's face with the emergency caption: "Have you seen this asshole?"

Meanwhile, a live stream of "Keeping up with the Commadresses" showed the former husband of Commandress Roseanne, It, hanging upside down, asking for help to a room full of no-one.

A part of our famed bombing mission, It had not been able to join us in our subsequent escape into hiding. He had been apprehended by female guards, and played dead.

The ruse worked. Commandress Roseanne took him to a taxidermist to have him stuffed and mounted on her wall.

Unbeknownst to the Commandress, the taxidermist stuffed It in ways that I can only fantasise about endlessly, and allowed It to continue his charade of playing dead - a ruse without much of an end-plan.

We followed the limo of the Commandress on CCTV, too. She was with her mother, the celebrity nurse, her latest Stud and her driver.

They had found Dud's discarded gown and presented it to their hunting dogs to pick up a scent.

They were close.

I intervened, removing the panels at the back of the shop and calling Dud into the darkness.

I lit a match.

"Hello, hello," I whispered. "Dud, follow the light."

*

Dud strained his eyes in the darkness.

"Stud Ramrod?" he asked.

"Welcome home, General."

"Stud Ramrod, is that you? I almost didn't recognise you."

"That's because I am now a raging homosexual," I boomed, proudly and gayly, slighty louder than I had intended.

"No, it's because you've grown an outrageous beard."

Beard aside, I could tell it was going to take a while for Dud to adjust to seeing me as the flamboyant poofter that I now definitely was.

I would give him time.

"Come this way," I told him.

Sensing that Dud's escape had left him tired, I carried the baby under one arm, and I carried Dud under the other, through the passage between the rear wall of the book store, and to the haven of safety beyond.

We made it to the secret panel and I knocked three times.

It opened wide.
We entered, and I announced to the boys:
"The saviour hath returned!"

114

CHAPTER EIGHTEEN

THE MAN CAVE

The troops lined up to greet He Who Was Certain To Lead Us To Triumph.

"First up, here's Cyborg Longun, engineered from the crippled body of Stud Longun, pulled from the wreckage of his plane, upgraded by myself with an in-built virtual map, a holographic generator projecting an image of himself up to three feet away, and a beard."

"Great to see you, Dud. Look what I can do now," Cyborg Longun beamed.

Longun pressed a button on the projector strapped around his neck and a holographic image of himself appeared three feet away.

"Why would you want to do that?" asked Dud.

"I don't know why. And look, a map that tells you where you are in the world, as long as you have wifi," Longun boasted, revealing the tablet screen I'd pasted to his chest.

"Why the beard?" Dud asked.

"Dud, I'm gay. Get over it." I explained. It was really going to take a while to get through to him on this issue.

"I'm gayer than a bishop in a barn dance."

"So, what we have here is Stud Longun with a projector round his neck, a tablet stuck to his chest and a strap-on beard," Dud concluded.

"Next up, the Transylvanian beast-man, former maid to Commandress Roseanne, Marku."

"It both pleases and surprises me to see you," whined Marku, in his usual winsome yet sinister tones.

"And under this beard, you know Stud Mastall. But not in the way I know him. Biblically. Because I'm gay." I told Dud. "Fellow grocery shopper with Longun and yourself. The love of my life. The man I long to marry. Strengths: surveillance tech. Weaknesses: sleep apnea."

"You're both gay?" Dud observed.

"I'm bi-curious," Stud Mastall claimed, coquettishly.

"Bi-curious: am I gay or am I super gay?" I teased. "Two men with beards, locked in an embrace, kissing. Could there be a more beautiful sight in nature?"

"And this has nothing to do with you living in a rather off-putting, fascist, female-centric state," Dud pointed out.

"That's right, it has nothing to do with that, and everything to do with the sweet smell of another man's breath," I confirmed.

"Right," Dud agreed, fully. "And Chef Niko?"

"Didn't make it," I admitted. "Technically, none of us knew how to fly or land planes safely. But we sure bombed this city good, like you told us."

"I told you that under no circumstances should you resort to violence. I said that you should fix the city's plumbing to demonstrate the worth of men."

"Right, but we read between the lines."

"What lines?" Dud wailed, gesticulating wildly to make us all laugh.

It was great to have him back.

*

"It looks like I'm not the only one with some introducing to do," I hinted.

Every man has a weakness. For me, that weakness was the comfort of another man's armpit.

As for Dud, it seemed that his weakness was the little person wearing novelty glasses, or more accurately, his protective feelings towards this unconvincing clone.

It was this feeling of protectiveness that the Commandress had preyed upon.

His sympathy for the child made him vulnerable.

I would never father a child, of course. This was another reason I was proud, and relieved, to be a flaming homosexual.

"Read this," said Dud, handing me a letter.

I read out loud to the boys:

"Dear Dud Wimpole, wherever you are, I have news for you. We conceived a child together. I worry about what will happen to him, and to me, after he's born. Please help him, Dud. He needs you. I hope he is kind like you are. Love, Nicolette."

It was a magnificent and convincing piece of writing.

Marku wiped a tear from his eye.

"Who'd have thought that Nicolette, the lipsticked limo driver, would write such a moving letter," Cyborg Longun observed.

"That was sent by Commandress Roseanne to trick me into coming back," Dud explained. "She told me so, herself. She also told me that the child is yours, Stud Ramrod."

"Mine? It couldn't be mine. I never slept with Nicollete," I pointed out.

Dud looked dumbfounded.

"Sure, the Commandress wanted us to conceive a child that she could claim as her own, and gain political prestige. I was in Nicolette's bedroom. I saw her perfect, gently curvaceous, supple female body lying there on the bed and I thought to myself, there's no doubt about it, I'd much rather be spooning up against a sweaty, hairy backed male. It was then that I realised this heterosexuality charade wasn't for me."

"A crushing disappointment," Marku whined.

"On the contrary, it was a beautiful night," I recalled. "Have you ever had one of those nights where you just stay awake together and talk for hours? I opened up about my newly awoken feelings, while she entertained herself in the bathroom by shoving plastic into her body."

"Well, then who is the father?" Mastall asked.

"A girl like that has many suitors." I suggested. "It could be anyone. It could even be Marku."

"She did not sleep with I," Marku admitted. "I tried, one fateful evening. I decided I would win her over. I bought her flowers. I stood outside her window, with the flowers, but it rained and she did not let me in. And so I bought new trousers. I stood outside her window, in my trousers. But it rained, and she did not let me in. I loved her."

"All that's in the past," I interjected, trying to provide the welcome befitting our returning, soon to be conquering hero. "You're back, Dud Wimpole. You're here. That's all that matters. Let me show you around."

*

"You gave us hope that a place like this could be possible, Dud," Mastall said, as we showed Dud the pad. "Wasn't it fun, our little escape attempts, when we had that silly hope that freedom was achievable?"

"It is achievable," Dud replied, without missing a beat.

"See? That's why he's the leader!" Longun chimed in.

"I'm not a leader. We have to take responsibility for our own actions," Dud proclaimed.

"That's exactly the kind of thing a leader would say," I pointed out, as I continued the tour.

I was pretty darn proud of the place.

It had your standard living room seating set. Reclinable chairs. Coffee table. Mini-fridge. Flat screen TV.

Over there was the monitoring desk: a bunch of screens on which we channeled every CCTV, city-cam or live TV feed in Dileag. Our eyes and ears on the outside world.

There was the pool table.

Dud sat the baby up there while I explained the colour choices of our furnishings.

The baby amused himself by clicking the balls together, and trying to throw himself off the edge of the table to his death three or four times a minute.

Great fun.

The walls were decorated with remnants of our past lives. These were things we'd managed to salvage on our clandestine raids into the city when we were setting up the place.

We'd found wicker baskets, the type the Studs used to shop with, street signs, traffic lights, red tunics, sports memorabilia. Hell, we'd even found the hang-gliders once used by Dud to try and lead an escape from the city.

Our walls were like a mural tribute to the past, and they gave us comfort.

There was a full working bar, and a DJ deck. Marku had discovered a skill for mixing both cocktails and Vinyl LP's.

Simultaneously!

The centre piece in our Man Cave was the tank we'd

commandeered amid the chaos and the rubble.

We'd driven it in through what used to be a delivery hatch for the mall, before we filled that up with concrete.

We'd turned the interior of the tank into a love making nest for me and Mastall.

The outside of the tank, my better half had decorated in potted plants and ribbons.

"And over here's a knitting corner for the gays," I told Dud.

"Aren't you perpetrating a number of stereotypes?"

"Yes," I said proudly. "Let me show you my baking kitchen"

"Cupcakes?" asked Dud.

"And grenades," I told him. "We've gotta be prepared."

"Are you going to live here?" Cyborg Longun asked, hopefully.

"I see that there's a need for us to have a place where we can be ourselves: a space," Dud began, thoughtfully. "But this is a cave. We're hiding. Don't you think there's something wrong about that?"

"You see? That is why he's the leader!" I cheered.

"I'm no leader," Dud quipped.

"Dud, some leaders lead by giving commands. Others lead by example. You're a lead by example kind of guy," Mastall observed, reminding me of why I had chosen him as my future husband.

"Our leader has returned and he will lead the revolution!" I cried.

The boys let out a mighty roar.

Dud pulled up a white-board and began to work on a strategy of how to entertain the baby.

The boys and I drank beer and played video games.

It was awesome!

CHAPTER NINETEEN

RACE!

It took around another hour for the women to find us.

We were still engrossed in the excellent video game, "Final Call of Action," which allows players to run around on a screen and shoot each other, when Marku got up to fix us some snacks.

His eyes must have caught a glimpse of our surveillance screens because he froze and said:

"We're found."

The rest of us gathered around the screens.

One screen displayed a live stream from outside the mall.

Decrepit, octogenarian women in combat outfits disembarked army vehicles and surrounded the building.

"Who are they?" Dud asked.

"The army," Stud Mastall explained. "It was observed that under the patriarchies, no female pensioner was admitted to join the fighting corps…"

"Corrective discrimination, got it," Dud concluded.

A black van circled the building.

"That's the reality TV crew following me around," Dud pointed out.

"Leading by example," Cyborg Longun observed, admiringly.

Another screen displayed CCTV footage from inside the mall of a gang of shaven headed security guards following the lead search group.

The lead group consisted of the stars and producers of "Keeping Up With the Commandreses:"

Chief Commandress Germaine, Commandress Roseanne, Commandress Nurse Vera, Stud Buffcheeks, and their non-driver, Chantelle.

Commandress Roseanne held the reins of a group of guard dogs. The dogs were foaming at the mouths. Poodles. Pink. Vicious.

The pack of poodles led the group to the back of the book shop.

"They've picked up our scent!" Cyborg Longun cried.

"Heightened sense of smell," Dud explained. "They're ovulating."

There was a knock at the door.

Marku, still frozen to the spot, screamed, flinging his hands into the air in surrender.

"They've found the secret panel," Stud Mastall exclaimed. "How?"

"You stuck a sign saying secret panel on the door," Dud pointed out.

I am a man.

I believe a man should own his mistakes.

"I've doomed us all," I confessed.

*

We managed to get the tank fired up just in time for the Commandresses, as they entered the Man Cave, to see us burst through the side wall.

We smashed through into the make-up section of Gracy's.

Shoppers dived out of the way screaming.

Crushing every counter in our way, the tank smashed through the next wall, rocking us all, Dud, the baby, Mastall, Longun and me, like nuts shaken in a can.

Marku remained behind in the Man Cave, frozen to the spot, hands in the air, unmoveable.

"Woohoo!" I cried, steering the tank through a shoe store.

They were having a sale.

We smashed that sale.

And the next wall - that was the outer shell of the mall.

We smashed through that, too.

"Couldn't you have reversed the way you came in?" Dud called from the back.

"Smash!" I explained.

We were free.

*

I steered the tank down the middle of a city centre street, cranking up the speed.

"How can we get this thing to the city gate?" Dud asked, tapping feverishly on Cyborg Longun's chest map.

"I don't know, I can't get a signal," Longun cried.

Then, opening the hatch, Cyborg Longun poked his head out the top of the tank.

"What's the diagnosis?" I called.

His answer was as incoherent as it was terrifying.

"We got skin-headed guards rounding the corner in a

monster truck," Longun reported. "They're hanging out the sides. They seem to have automatic rifles. Oh darn."

"What's oh darn?" Mastall asked.

"Poodles. We got ovulating poodles on our tail. They're gaining!" Longun cried.

"Where are we?" Dud called up.

And Longun confirmed:

"We're in the shit"

CHAPTER TWENTY

BOOM!

The pitter patter of tiny ovulating poodle paws sprinkled across the roof of the tank.

"They're onboard!" Cyborg Longun called.

"Close the hatch!" I shouted.

"No, I'll handle them," the crazy bastard shouted back.

Cyborg Longun climbed up onto the roof, ducking to avoid a pink poodle flying straight for his jugular.

"Longun, watch out!" Dud cried.

"It's ok. I've been patched up once before, I can get patched up again. Take care of your son!"

With that, the brave Cyborg Longun fired up his holographic projector and a mirror image of himself appeared three feet away.

The dozen or so poodle pack ignored the hologram completely and went straight for Longun himself.

"There, there puppies," Longun screamed, closing the hatch with his foot.

The next we saw of him, Cyborg Longun had fallen off the tank, swarmed in balls of pink fur.

The monster truck trailing us swerved to avoid the mound of rabid cuteness and we in the tank sped on.

*

I began to lose consciousness.

"What's that smell?" I asked.

"I need to change his pamper," Dud called.

"I can't breathe," I cried.

The streets of Dileag swirled ahead of me in a dizzying blur.

"Not on the satin sheets!" Mastall wailed.

Dud climbed onto the roof of the tank, holding the gaseous child at a distance.

"Throw me a spare pamper," Dud called to Mastall from above.

My head spinning, I manoeuvred the tank around the city stadium.

A flood of disconnected images blurred my vision: the road ahead, clouds, the stadium notice board reading "Morning ceremony topic: Toxics are Trouble!"

"I need wipes! Give me more wipes!" I heard Dud screaming.

Behind us, the monster truck guard vehicle gained ground.

The city gates loomed up ahead: huge wooden monuments to imprisonment.

It was now or never.

I pushed the tank up to full speed.

*

The tank smashed through the city gates in an explosion of noise and splinter.

Karash!

Wooden remnants of the monoliths reigned down upon us.

Then I remembered Dud, still up there on the roof with the child.

"Dud, are you ok?" I called up.

"I need rash cream," the great man called back.

The land outside the city gates was dry, arid, orange.

I sped the tank on, churning up a cloud of dust behind us.

From that orange cloud, they emerged: our nightmare.

Mastall, at the viewfinder, reported on the horrors that followed us.

The monster guard truck, followed by army trucks, driven by pensioners, joined by an eighteen wheeler freight truck, accentuating evil; all were in pursuit and gaining ground.

In the cabin of the eighteen wheeler, Commandress Roseanne drove, chewing and spitting; Chantelle sat beside her, playing with her phone, uninterested. Commandress Nurse Vera sat on the lap of Stud Buffcheeks, brandishing medical instruments.

Chief Commandress Germaine leaned out of the side of the cabin, holding onto the door with one hand, her other - a blade.

The camera crew truck drove alongside the eighteen wheeler, filming Chief Commandress Germaine with her black cloak billowing in the wind,

At that moment, the wind caught the used pamper on the roof of our tank.

The pamper flew through the air in a gust of gas and grime and splattered into the windshield of the eighteen wheeler.

Dud climbed down from the roof with the baby.

"All done," he said.
I was in the presence of a genius.

CHAPTER TWENTY ONE

A HERO IS BORN

"Fresh as a daisy," Dud continued, as he rejoined us in the tank.

We powered on, being pursued by half of Dileag - the easily angered half - in a monster truck, army vans and an eighteen wheeler.

The monster truck reached us first. Shaven headed guards hung out the side and fired their pistols at the tank.

"It'll take more than that to harm us," Mastall boasted, and both he and I laughed uproariously.

"They've got a bazooka," Dud pointed out (not laughing), as the guards loaded up an anti-tank rocket launcher.

"I'll deal with this," announced Stud Mastall, climbing onto the roof. "Hand me that box of grenades."

Dud groaned under the weight, drawing on all his might to lift a fully loaded cardboard box from the floor of the tank into Mastall's arms.

"Dud, these are Marku's cupcakes," Mastall called down, as bullets whizzed past his head.

It turned out that in our haste to take all we could from the Man Cave, we had forgotten a few essentials.

"I'm gonna go introduce myself to the guards," my beloved Mastall announced, casting an erotic glance my way.

I saw him through the roof hatch, making his way to the side of the tank, steadying himself.

Just before the guards could fire their bazooka, Mastall leapt onto their vehicle.

The monster truck careened to the side in a cloud of dust and from within that cloud, there was a mighty explosion.

"I'm going to marry that man, some day," I cheered, as we sped on.

*

"Cliff-top, straight ahead!" Dud called. "Do the radios work?"

"Why, you want to dance?" I asked.

The army vans drew level on the left of the tank, keeping apace.

At the front of the lead army truck, strapped to the fender, an 80 year old corporal was playing a rock riff on a violin.

It really was a fun time for all.

The army leader, as old and as withered as they come, stepped from the lead van onto the tank roof.

"That's Commandress General Nancy," Dud explained. "She seems to have come out of retirement for the occasion. I'll politely ask her and the army to leave us alone."

It was an excellent plan.

Dud set the baby down in the navigator's seat and

climbed to the roof.

"Been avoiding me, have you?" screamed the decrepit, mad old woman, standing on the roof - as the tank hurtled towards the cliff's edge.

She raised her right hand, high above her head, signalling Dud to take it.

Dud obliged.

She raised her left. Dud took it. They were locked in combat, the two leaders, Dud Wimpole, and the frail and withered old woman.

It was a battle of the brawn, a test of strength, a clash of the Titans.

Dud was losing, so I steadied the tank to rumble on in a straight line.

Dud dropped to one knee. Then another.

"I'd better handle the grandmas, Dud," I suggested, grabbing the General and tossing her over my shoulder.

Dud scrambled back through the hatch to take the controls.

I leapt into the nearest army van with the General over my shoulder, tearing through the canopy, and barging into the awaiting combat pensioners in the back.

The sheer momentum caused the van to careen to the left, taking out those vehicles to its side like dominos, before losing traction, rising into the air and spinning wildly.

And then all went black.

*

When I came to, the dust had settled.

Broken vehicles, mangled metal and irate grannies lay strewn across the ground.

The tank had come to a stop at the cliff-top.

Behind it, the eighteen wheeler, the film crew van, and what was left of the army convoy had pulled up.

Chief Commandress Germaine, blade in hand, flanked by her daughter, inspected the tank.

The film crew caught every moment.

The Chief Commandress turned to her group and her face said it all. Dud Wimpole was gone.

Attention turned to the cliff-top.

Surely not?

Chief Commandress Germaine led her cronies to the edge of the cliff and there they stood, frozen, looking down.

Unable to resist the urge to see what they saw, no matter how gruesome, no matter how final, I raced to the edge of the cliff, myself.

And there, hang-gliding through the air, like a bespectacled eagle, the Baby Dud strapped to his chest, was…

Well, it was Dud Wimpole.

"Yahaaa!" I heard myself scream in triumph, rapturous with excitement, and uncaring as shaven-headed guards from the eighteen wheeler took me by the arms, and dragged me to an army van.

Some way out to sea, a cargo vehicle hovered a few feet above the water.

Its Captain waited on deck, for it was there that Dud was heading, and to freedom.

A transport platform - no bigger than a raft - waited at an equal distance between the ship and the cliff-top, where Dud would land, beautifully, gracefully, as though destiny called.

But in that moment, and perhaps forever more, I felt that I was up there with him, wind blowing through my hair, gliding through the sky, escaping, free.

Dud Wimpole.
What a man!

EPILOGUE

SHOW'S NOT OVER

By Cargo

So, Dud Wimpole lands on the hover-raft, some way between me on the cargo ship and the crowd on the cliff-top.

It was all going to plan.

I'd kept a check on Dud's movements on Dileag. It was hard not to once he was part of a high profile reality tv show and media onslaught.

But when Dud called me on his old island transmitter, telling me he was hiding out in some kind of man-cave and that shit was about to go down, I knew I had to be there.

This is how it goes down.

Dud unstraps himself from some kind of gliding contraption and all that's left is for me to bring him and the mini-Dud to the ship.

But then, Commandress Roseanne's mother, the Chief Commandress Germaine, she gets a megaphone, see? And she calls out:

"Dud Wimpole. Oh, Dud Wimpole. Aren't you

forgetting something?"

And then one of her cronies opens up the back of a freight truck.

Around two hundred pale, malnourished, frightened children leave the vehicle, chained to each other in small groups.

They join Chief Commandress Germaine at the cliff-top.

Dud looks back in horror.

Chief Commandress Germaine continues over the megaphone.

"These represent the last of the children of Dileag. These are the children whose deaths you will be responsible for, if you do not surrender, and return to Dileag and marry my beautiful daughter."

Dud gulps.

He looks out to sea at my ship, at escape, and back to the children, and down to the baby Dud.

"What'll it be, Dud Wimpole?" Chief Commandress Germaine asks, edging the children forward to the cliff edge.

*

Dud hugs the baby and places him down at one end of the raft.

I know what I have to do next.

I hit the remote and the raft splits in two, Dud Wimpole at one end, the baby at the other.

I press another button and half the raft starts heading my way - the half carrying the baby.

The other half starts moving back towards the cliff-face - the half carrying Dud Wimpole.

One half of the raft reaches my ship.

I climb down the ladder and pull up the baby Dud.

I climb back into the ship, holding him in my arms.

*

I don't see why the Commandresses let Dud send the baby off like that.

Maybe they felt indifferent to the child.

Maybe they were too consumed with catching Dud.

Maybe they were giddy with the prospect of an imminent marriage.

The baby wasn't part of the deal, after all. Dud returns. They let the children of Dileag live.

Whatever their reasons for letting the baby Dud go, they never would have foresaw the epic repercussions their oversight would have on the future of mankind.

As for, Dud Wimpole, well...

He climbs onto the hanging platform at the bottom of the cliff.

As Dud is pulled up the side of the cliff on the crate platform, he looks our way.

He raises his hand and gives a sweeping wave.

The baby Dud raises his little hand and waves back.

It is their farewell.

I trigger the engines and the ship rises a few more feet off the ocean surface.

Dud reaches the top of the cliff.

Shaven headed guards hold him by the arms and bundle him into the back of a van.

The convoy turns away from the cliff-top and begins the trip back to Dileag: a fleet of trucks, a pack of armoured vehicles and a chain of vans:

One of them containing Dud Wimpole.

THE END

NOTES

1. Must buy eggs!

2. Remember that the tap in the downstairs bathroom is broken. Keep it turned to the left.

QUOTES

"Now? Now you really can't pursue someone further than, 'No'. It's like, 'OK, cool'. But then there's the, 'Oh why'd you give up?' And it's like, 'Well, because I didn't want to go to jail?'"

Henry (Superman) Cavill

"I just wanted to apologise for any confusion and misunderstanding that this may have created. Insensitivity was absolutely not my intention."

Henry (Superman) Cavill

"The people are tired of liberty."

Mussolini

"In light of this I would just like to clarify and confirm to all that I have always and will continue to hold women in the highest of regard. Never would I intend to disrespect women in any way, shape or form."

Henry (Superman) Caville

"We need to reshape our own perception of how we view ourselves. We have to step up as women and take the lead."

Beyonce Knowles

"The more successful I become, the more I need a man." Beyonce Knowles "If he invited you out, he's got to pay."

Beyonce Knowles

"I can't deal with someone needing space."

Taylor Swift

"Women have to take the time to focus on our mental health — take time for self, for the spiritual, without feeling guilty or selfish."

Beyoncé Knowles

"I think about food literally all day every day. It's a thing."

Taylor Swift

"The great thing about McDonald's is that they have a lot of different things on the menu. I love their salads."

Beyonce Knowles

"The thing women have yet to learn is nobody gives you power. You just take it."

Roseanne Barr

"The question isn't who's going to let me; it's who is going to stop me."

Ayn Rand

"Have a power piece in your wardrobe. If it's the one dress that makes you feel so badass, or the one crisp button-down — whatever it is so that when you wake up on those days where you're not really feeling going into work, you put that piece on and it's almost like your own anthem. It can really shift the energy of your whole day."

Meghan Markle

"My version of Superman is essentially of a guy who has spent his whole life alone."

Henry (Superman) Cavill

"The Lion King always makes me cry, especially when Simba's father gets trampled."

Vanessa Hudgens

"I think the biggest part of being a girl boss in the office, at home, or anywhere you go is just knowing your value . . . it's important to flex your intellectual prowess, even if you're wiggling around in a pencil skirt."

Meghan Markle

BOATS

An Index

The following boats appear in *Women on Top 2: The Testicles*, in alphabetical order:

Cargo's ship   p: 11

READING GROUP DISCUSSION POINTS

1. Despite being in a leadership position Commandress Roseanne is clearly oppressed. Who would you say oppresses her?

2. Dud Wimpole disappoints Commandress Roseanne sexually. In which other ways is Dud Wimpole a disappointment?

3. Cargo shows signs of autoerotica fixation, amongst other perversions. What's your favourite perversion?

4. In his narration, Stud Ramrod said of Dud Wimpole, "It was great to have him back?" What did he mean by this?

5. Dileag represents a religio-fascist state based on feminist ideals. What are your thoughts on McDonald's McMuffins?

6. By the year 2030, China's one-child policy and its cultural preference for male heirs will have created a society overrun by 30 million unmarriageable men. Who will tell them what to do?

Dud Wimpole will not return, in *Women on Top: Freesome*

ALSO AVAILABLE

PRISON BREAK!

From the creators of *ODD*, it's time to take a *Prison Break!*

Struggling with life on the outside, three disenfranchised, emasculated males decide to escape by breaking into prison.

It was the most secure prison in the world, but they were determined to break in.

The feature length screenplay.

SMALL MAN COMPLEX

He's not a little boy; he's a little man.

When average Tom Manginer is afflicted by an embarrassing shrinking condition, he compensates with a massive, debilitating small man complex.

Available for the first time, the full length feature film screenplay.

With an introduction by Tom Cruise.

ODD

When a pandemic of Oppositional Defiant Disorder afflicts the male population of the world, women must work together to save humanity. It's a disaster movie.

In the first quarter of the year 2022, the motion picture, *ODD*, was filmed with an estimated budget of $240 million.

The film was screened once, at the Westwood Village Theatre.

Following the screening, the single known print of the movie was burned at the request of the studio.

This is the screenplay.

THE ANKLE PROBLEM

What is the problem?

Marcus seems to have it all, a great job, a nice house and a good bunch of friends he plays football with at the weekends.

Plus he's married his beloved Amy, and they've just got back from their honeymoon.

But in the weeks after the marriage, nobody sees Marcus. No friends, no football, no Marcus.

He says he has an ankle problem, but can this be the whole story?

How did he injure his ankle while on honeymoon?

How does his ankle prevent him from going out for a drink?

And what's that unearthly sound of something cracking coming from his house?

It turns out, Marcus may have a bigger problem than his ankle.

NOBLES: THE MUSICAL

In the tradition of *Walden*, *Oblomov* and *Les Miserables*, comes *Nobles: The Musical!*

The post-pandemic world has seen a reluctance amongst the workforce to return to work. Schemes such as furlough, government subsidies and work-from-home have made non-engagement in work the norm.

Coupled with this is the perhaps tone deaf, multi-million pound coronation of King Charles III, unprecedented profits for supermarkets and energy companies monopolising essential services, and cultural emphasis on personal wellbeing.

However, for a group of friends in one seafront arcade coffee shop, the life of non-work is nothing new.

Using an expert knowledge of the UK welfare system, a philosophical adherence to non-participation and a carefully cultivated lack of skills, the Nobles have managed to avoid work for going on half a century.

And tonight, they're going to sing about it.

164

165

168

174